making scented
soap

60 fragrant soaps
and bath bombes
to make at home

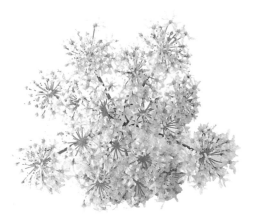

Linda Hamblen

COLLINS & BROWN

To all budding soap makers who share a
fondness for the natural world.

First published in hardback in Great Britain in 2003
First published in paperback in Great Britain in 2005 by
Collins & Brown Ltd
The Chrysalis Building
Bramley Road, London W10 6SP

An imprint of **Chrysalis** Books Group plc

Distributed in the United States and Canada by Sterling Publishing Co.
387 Park Avenue South, New York NY 10016

Project Manager: Nicola Hodgson
Editor: Katie Hardwicke
Proofreader: Michele Turney
Indexer: Margaret Binns
Designer: Caroline Hillier
Photography: Siân Irvine

Reproduced by Classicscan Pte, Singapore
Printed by Kyodo Printing Co Ltd, Singapore

Important Notice
The publishers have made every effort to ensure that all instructions given in this book are accurate
and safe, but they cannot accept liability, whether direct or consequential and however arising. If you
are pregnant or have any known or suspected allergies – or are acutely sensitive to particular plants,
oils, dyes, herbs, spices, or other substances – you may want to consult a doctor about possible
adverse reactions before undertaking the projects in this book. Techniques and materials in this book
are not for children.

WA2

making scented
soap

contents

the science of scent

Our sense of smell is perhaps the most powerful of our senses, evoking all manner of emotions and memories. One wisp of lingering perfume can transport us back to a long forgotten memory, place, event, or person. But why is this sense of smell so important and why do plants emit such intoxicating and powerful aromas?

In times past our sense of smell was our basic survival instinct, our early warning of friend or foe, or our natural detection of edible or poisonous plants. Research has shown that we are 10,000 times more sensitive to smell than we are to taste.

Perfume acts as a survival instinct for plants too, attracting pollinating insects, butterflies and bees with a bribe of sweet-scented nectar. As they travel, feeding on nectar, insects transfer pollen from plant to plant, thus ensuring the future of the next generation of seeds. Interestingly, plants pollinated by the wind or by birds produce little perfume. They don't need to, as the wind blows regardless and birds have a very poor sense of smell.

Through various distillation and extraction processes it is possible to capture these plant aromas, producing what is known as an essential oil. Often referred to as the very essence of the plant, essential oils have been used both medicinally and as perfumes for thousands of years. Frankincense, myrrh, and sandalwood all have a documented history of some 4000 years of use. These oils were highly prized. Trade routes were established, crossing continents, and whole economies were dependent on the production of a single oil. These days, many oils are still used medically, therapeutically, and in the aromatherapy and perfume trade.

The aim of this book is to take these natural aromas and combine them with the traditional craft of cold processed soap making, creating an array of beautiful and aromatic herbal soaps. The emphasis throughout is on natural ingredients and plant and vegetable oils with infusions of herbs and spices and flower petals. Floral, citrus, herbal, spicy, and woody, each chapter concentrates on a particular scent note – the five basic categories by which perfume is traditionally described.

If you find cold processed soap making a little too daunting at first, start with one of the easier recipes using a soap base (a liquid soap or a clear soap). You'll find this type of soap making surprisingly simple and very rewarding, with satisfying results each time. As your confidence and understanding of the materials grow, move on to one of the simpler cold processed recipes and before long your imagination will be your only limitation as you create your own recipes.

Although this book contains predominantly soap recipes, you will also find a small selection of recipes for bath bombes and massage melts plus all the information you will need to give you the confidence to design your own fragrant and natural treats.

Happy soap making.

ingredients

& techniques

tools and equipment

Most of the equipment you will need can be found among your everyday kitchen utensils. Glass, most plastics, and stainless steel items are ideal for soap making, but do not use anything wooden or aluminum as the lye solution (sodium hydroxide dissolved in water) reacts with them both.

Cups or jugs, mixing bowls, and saucepans should be large enough to accommodate all your ingredients with room to spare to allow for ease of stirring without the risk of any overspill. Again, use plastic or stainless steel spoons for stirring the lye and soap solution. Containers used to hold the lye solution should be heatproof as the reaction

between water and sodium hydroxide creates a lot of heat and the solution and utensils will get very hot. Make sure that your utensils are kept solely for soap making and don't use them for food again afterward. Goggles, gloves, a face mask, and apron are also essential.

Good quality, accurate measuring scales are a key piece of equipment and ideally should weigh in $1/12$ ounce (1 gram) increments. Your scales should have a bowl large enough to accommodate a pint, or half a liter, of liquid. Liquids are measured in weight rather than volume to maintain consistent and accurate measurements.

basic equipment

1. scales with large bowl suitable for weighing liquids
2. stainless steel saucepans
3. stainless steel double boiler
4. heatproof measuring cup with a spout or jug
5. large mixing bowl
6. stainless steel measuring spoons
7. glass pipette or dropper for measuring essential oils
8. stainless steel or plastic spoon and slotted spoon
9. cook's thermometer

In addition to the basic equipment, you may need a hand grater for grating leftover soap or a block of clear soap base. A pestle and mortar or food processor will be useful for grinding leaves and herbs.

Plastic tubs make ideal molds. Margarine tubs, sandwich spread pots, and yogurt cartons all offer exciting possibilities. You can even make your own simple wooden or cardboard molds. Line them with a plastic bag first then pour your soap mix straight in. When set, remove the bag from the mold and carefully peel away from the soap.

A variety of shapes and sizes of molds is used for the recipes in this book. If your mixture is too much for one tub, use two. If you have any left over, pour it into a margarine tub or yogurt pot. It doesn't matter if the soap is in a variety of molds; it won't affect the quality of the final bar, and you can slice it into any shape or size you want once cured. A solid plastic tube, such as a length of drainpipe, sealed at one end, makes an ideal mold for round soaps. Simply cut the soap into rounds once it has cured.

Each recipe produces approximately 2 lb (1 kg) of soap, which yields about ten 3½ oz (100 g) bars. Follow either imperial or metric measurements for each recipe, never a mixture of the two.

10	plastic molds
11	sharp knife for slicing bars
12	pestle and mortar
13	oil spray
14	graters
15	spatulas
16	cookie cutters
17	clips
18	whisks
19	sieve
20	goggles, gloves, and mask
21	funnel
	blankets or towels for insulating the soap as it sets

base oils

The recipes in this book call for the use of many different plant and vegetable oils. Each oil imparts its own unique quality. Some have therapeutic properties, while others add color or texture. Some make a harder or softer bar of soap, some produce a rich lather, and others silky, creamy bubbles. This list gives you a little more insight and helps you understand each oil's specific characteristics. Combined with the saponification chart on page 26, you can use the information below to give you the confidence to design your own recipes.

avocado Nourishes and restores dry and mature skin. A rich, heavy oil, high in unsaponifiables (see page 26) so, added in small quantities to your recipe, helps make a very moisturizing soap. Use up to 10–15% in your own recipe.

beeswax Adds the sweet scent of honey to your recipes. Added to soaps and melts it makes a harder, firmer bar. Only a small amount is needed in cold processed soap making, a maximum of 5%, otherwise it will inhibit the lathering qualities of your soap.

borage Pressed from the seed of the borage flower, a clear, odorless liquid that is very moisturizing and soothing to sensitive skin. Use up to 10–15% in your own recipe.

castor A thick, clear, viscous liquid pressed from the castor bean. A very moisturizing, lubricating oil, high in fatty acids. Acts as a humectant, attracting moisture to the skin. Use up to 20% in your recipes to produce a wonderfully emollient, hard bar of soap with lots and lots of lather.

chocolate Choose a chocolate that has a high cocoa butter content, ideally at least 80%, with little sugar added. Chocolate will add a rich dark color to your soaps and melts with the same benefits as cocoa butter. Only include a small percentage in your recipe, maximum of 10%, otherwise your soaps will have a dirty brown lather.

cocoa butter Pressed from the cocoa bean, cocoa butter has a rich, chocolatey aroma, and softening, skin-healing properties. A deodorized cocoa butter is also available. A hard, white, brittle fat that adds firmness to melts and makes a hard bar of soap. Use at no more than 15% in combination with softer oils or your soaps will be prone to cracking.

coconut Obtained from copra, the dried "meat" of the coconut. Produces a very hard soap with a lovely, fluffy lather so add to all your recipes. Best used in combination with other oils but can be used anything up to 100% in your recipes. Soap made entirely from coconut oil is called "mariner's soap," as it is the only soap that will still lather in salt water.

cucumber extract A clear, viscous liquid that is cooling and soothing. Just a couple of teaspoonfuls in your recipes is all you need for perfect summertime soaps.

honey Sweetly scented, softening, and moisturizing. Honey is a humectant, attracting moisture to your skin to help make it soft and supple. For a formula for dry and cracked skin, add a teaspoonful to your recipe.

jojoba Jojoba oil is a liquid wax, similar in composition to the oil our skin naturally secretes. Quickly absorbed, it helps restore elasticity to the skin while nourishing and soothing. Suitable for young and sensitive skins. A maximum of 5% is all your recipes will need.

milk Both goat's milk or milk powder will add wonderful, softening, and soothing properties to your soaps. If using fresh milk, you can substitute all or part of your lye liquid for milk, but do make sure that it is ice cold before adding the sodium hydroxide (preferably freeze it until it is of a slushy consistency). If using milk powder you can simply add a couple of teaspoonfuls (10 ml) at the trace stage.

olive Various grades of olive oil are available, ranging from extra virgin, the first pressing of the fruit, to pomace, the final pressing of the ground flesh and pits. All grades make a lovely, gentle, emollient soap. Pomace is the cheapest and lowest grade oil, although it tends to trace more quickly than higher grades of olive oil. Your soap recipes should all contain a high percentage of olive oil to add firmness and a silkiness to the lather. Castile soap is made from 100% olive oil.

palm Produced from the pulp and flesh of the fruit of the oil palm. High in fatty acids and a rich source of beta-carotene, producing a bright, buttercup yellow when added to soaps and melts. Saponifies quickly to produce a nice, hard soap that doesn't dissolve quickly in water. White palm has all the properties of unrefined yellow palm oil without the color. Use anything up to 100% palm oil in your recipes.

pumpkin A rich dark oil with a nutty aroma, pressed from ripe pumpkin seeds. High in vitamins and minerals but its main use is to add color to your soaps and melts. Just a few teaspoonfuls will create a delicate green color in melts, while a maximum of 5–10% included in your soap recipes will give a rich, honey brown.

rosehip Grows wild in the southern Andes. The amber seeds are cold-pressed to produce an oil rich in

vitamins and minerals. Has been shown to reduce scarring and induce skin healing. Invaluable for a number of sensitive skin problems. Expensive, so only use 5–10% in your soaps, but you'll find rosehip oil a very worthwhile emollient. Only use in melts if you are going to use them straight away as this oil can turn rancid quickly.

shea butter Expressed from the pits of the fruit of the African butter tree and also known as African Karite butter. Smooth and creamy white butter that melts to the slightest touch. Extremely moisturizing and gentle, gives a luxurious, silky feel to melts and soaps. Add 5–10% to your own soap recipes.

sunflower A light oil suitable for dry, delicate skins. Less expensive than olive oil. Slow to saponify, so use in conjunction with other more saturated oils. Produces a light lather with big, big bubbles. Limit sunflower oil to around 15% in your recipes to ensure a firm bar.

sweet almond A fabulous moisturizing oil, used by many aromatherapists as a base for massage blends. Softening and skin conditioning, it is suitable for both melts and soaps. It saponifies easily, producing a gentle soap with a good, mild lather. Can be used as one of the main ingredients in your soap recipe. Soap made from 100% almond oil is very pleasant, but for a more luxurious bar use in combination with olive, coconut, or palm oil.

walnut A pale, light oil pressed from the dry nuts. Excellent moisturizing and emollient qualities but a little slow to saponify, so only use up to 10% in a recipe.

wheat germ High in vitamin E, a natural preservative. Wheat germ is a thick, sticky oil that helps nourish dry and cracked, mature skin. The refined oil lacks the penetrating odor of the complete oil. Avoid if you have a wheat allergy. A maximum of 10–15% is recommended in recipes.

From left, beeswax pellets, pumpkin oil, beeswax ingots, cocoa butter (back), white palm oil (front), sweet almond oil, olive oil, glycerine soap pellets, yellow palm, and chocolate.

botanicals

Add herbs, spices, and flower petals (botanicals) to your recipes to create texture, color, and enhance scent. Herbs can be used as a decorative topping, finely ground to add texture to your soaps, or infused in a tea to create a smooth, even color. Like all natural ingredients, many herb colors will fade a little with time, but your creations will prove so popular that they probably won't last long enough for this to happen!

Always try to buy organically grown herbs and spices, or why not harvest petals and leaves from your own garden? What nicer gift than a large chunk of soap, not only handmade, but handmade with your own home-grown herbs and flowers?

alkanet (*Alkanna tinctoria*) Alkanet can color your recipes anything from red to pink, and from purple to blue. In fact, alkanet is a good pH indicator of your recipe. For instance, the more fatty acids in your melt recipe, or citric acid in your bombes, the redder it will be. Soaps, by definition, are slightly alkaline so the alkanet will turn a bluey mauve color. Works well if used as a tea infusion in soaps.

basil (*Ocimum basilicum*) A tender herb, steeped in folklore. The dried and crumbled leaves of basil can be used to create a speckled greeny brown color in your recipes.

bladderwrack (*Fucus vesiculosus*) A salt scented seaweed that makes an attractive addition to soaps. Crush before use otherwise it may feel a little coarse to the touch, though it does soften quickly upon contact with water.

calendula petals (*Calendula officinalis*) Old English marigold. A bright, sunny orange flower, regarded as the emblem of love during medieval times. The flowers contain many skin healing properties as well as adding a golden orange color that is slow to fade.

cayenne pepper (*Capsicum* spp.) Adds a delicate salmon pink color to your recipes that doesn't fade too quickly. Just one teaspoonful of cayenne will turn your soaps a baby pink color; more will add a deeper, richer hue.

chocolate (*Theobroma cacao*) Powdered or melted chunks can both be added to your recipes.

cinnamon (*Cinnamomum zeylanicum*) Use the powder to create a warm, gentle brown in soaps, bombes, and melts, or use a piece of curled cinnamon bark as a decorative topping.

citrus peel (*Citrus* spp.) Finely grated, citrus peel adds delicate flecks to your creations as well as acting as a gentle exfoliant. Citrus slices also make an attractive topping. Add just before you are ready to pour your soaps into the mold as too much citrus peel may inhibit tracing.

clove buds (*Syzygium aromaticum*) Strongly scented with a sweet-spicy odor and a perfect topping to festive recipes. Clove can be a skin irritant.

coffee (*Coffea* spp.) Coffee is an effective natural deodorizer so is a good addition to kitchen soaps. Finely ground, coffee adds attractive flecks of color to your recipes but it may also be used as an infusion for a more even color.

frankincense (*Boswellia thurifera*) Both the "tears" and ground powder make an attractive addition to soaps, melts, and bombes. Frankincense and myrrh tears are the oleo-gum-resin harvested from the trees in a similar way to rubber tapping. They are then stem distilled to produce the essential oil.

indigo (*Indigofera tinctoria*) A shrubby plant, native to India, that for centuries has been fermented to produce a strong blue dye. You only need a few grains to color your soaps. Aim for a pale, marbled blue rather than a dark blue or you may end up with not only a blue lather, but blue hands too!

juniper berry (*Juniperus communis*) The dried berries of the juniper tree add an interesting textural effect to soaps as well as imparting their rich, deep color.

lavender buds (*Lavandula* spp.) Known since Roman times for its deodorant properties, lavender derives its name from the Latin word *lava,* meaning to wash. The azure blue buds make an attractive topping.

loofa (*Luffa cylindrical*) Makes a great natural exfoliator when added to soaps. The plants are easy to grow from seed, so, if you have a little space in your greenhouse or conservatory, you could grow your own.

myrrh (*Commiphora myrrha*) Similar to frankincense, but darker in color, myrrh powder adds a warm, pink-brown color to your creations. The mellow-scented tears look a little like brown sugar crystals.

nettle leaves (*Urtica dioica*) Stinging nettles. Traditionally used as a hair shampoo, they have a reputation for eliminating dandruff and preventing hair loss. Added to soap they create a pleasant green color.

paprika (*Capsicum annuum*) Creates a warm, rich red when added to soaps. Add only a touch to bombes, as too much will leave a red tide mark around your bath.

parsley (*Petroselinum crispum*) Use as a tea or simply mix in the powdered leaves. Parsley creates a light, apple green when added to soaps. The color will, unfortunately, fade but store your soaps away from direct sunlight to preserve the color for as long as possible.

poppy seeds (*Papaver somniferum*) White or blue poppy seeds are a good, scrubby exfoliator in soaps.

rose buds and rosehips (*Rosa* spp.) Make a very pretty topping on soaps, bombes, and melts. Ground rosehips add a delicate pinkish color to soaps that fades a little to an equally attractive pinky brown.

rose geranium (*Pelargonium graveolens*) Finely chopped and powdered leaves add a delicate green color to your soaps that fades with time to a yellowy green. Make sure that you use leaves from the scented, not the pot, geranium.

rosemary (*Rosmarinus officinalis*) The powdered leaves add a mossy green color to your recipes. Rosemary is also an antiseptic and effective hair tonic, adding a lustrous shine to dark hair.

safflower (*Carthamus tinctorius*) Also known as fake saffron, although the plant itself is no relation. The petals of the flowers are a deep orangey red, and hold their color well in soap. Mixed with powdered talc, the flowers are also used in the preparation of rouge.

soapwort (*Saponaria officinalis*) Small, delicately scented flowers with smooth, oval, deep-veined leaves. The leaves, stems, and roots are all high in natural saponins which, when boiled, make a gentle shampoo with a fine, delicate lather. Historically, this plant has also been used for cleaning wool and cloth. If you don't have the plant growing in your garden, both the dried leaves and root work equally well.

spirulina seaweed (*Spirulina* spp.) Spirulina has a very distinctive aroma – think of a sandy beach after the tide has gone out. Fortunately, its scent does fade quickly and can easily be disguised with a careful choice of essential oils. Added to soaps, it produces a rich green that fades to a warm, earthy green.

thyme (*Thymus vulgaris*) In the Middle Ages it was said that drinking a tea of thyme enabled one to see fairies, and traditionally tufts of thyme form one of the fairies' favorite abodes. The tiny green leaves of this magical plant add an attractive textural effect to soaps.

turmeric (*Curcuma longa*) Related to ginger, turmeric is made from the powdered rhizome. It will stain work surfaces and fingers so, like indigo, do not use in massage melts. However, added to soaps it makes a warm, peachy yellow.

walnut leaves (*Juglans regia*) Powdered leaves create a rich, dark greeny brown when added to soaps. Use crushed for a mottled, speckled effect.

wheat germ (*Triticum vulgare*) A gentle exfoliator that softens and soothes sensitive skin. The tiny flakes make a very attractive addition to your recipes too.

Botanicals used include, from back left, frankincense, citrus slices, rose hips, turmeric, cloves, wheat germ, myrrh and star anise.

essential oils

Essential oils are a natural ingredient, the very essence of the plant itself. Extracted from the flowers, fruit, leaves, bark, and roots of the plant, many oils have been used both for their scent and therapeutic qualities for thousands of years.

Some plants produce more than one type of oil. For example, the bitter orange tree (*Citrus aurantium*) produces three distinct oils: Neroli, or orange blossom, from the flowers; petitgrain from the leaves and twigs, and bitter orange from the almost ripe fruit.

The most common method of extracting the essential oils is via steam distillation. Steam is passed through the plant material, soaking up the essential oil as it goes. This aromatic vapor is then passed through a series of tubes, surrounded by cold water, which acts as a condenser. The condensed, distilled floral water is collected with the essential oil floating on the top. The essential oil is then siphoned off. The remaining floral water is a useful by-product, having a delicate, less intense scent than the oils. Floral waters are a useful addition to liquid soaps.

Read through this list before designing your own recipes. Generally you need to add between 2–3% essential oils by weight of your base oils. Peppermint needs a little less. Some light, highly volatile citrus oils may need a touch more. Experience will tell you how to fine-tune your recipe.

A final, brief word of caution: although essential oils have many therapeutic benefits, some are contra indicated and this list is not intended as a definitive guide.

almond, bitter (*Prunus dulcis*) This oil has a characteristic marzipan-like scent. It is extracted from the macerated kernels of the bitter almond tree. The maceration process forms prussic acid, otherwise known as cyanide! Before sale the oil is rectified to make it free from prussic acid (FFPA).

basil (*Ocimum basilicum*) A spicy, sweet green scent with a fresh, balsamic undertone. Extracted by steam distillation from the flowering herb. Avoid during pregnancy.

benzoin (*Styrax benzoin*) A viscous, orange-brown mass with a rich, sweet, balsamic scent, extracted from the trunk of styrax benzoin. Acts as a good fixative to other oils, particularly citrus. Use only in tiny amounts.

bergamot (*Citrus bergamia*) A light, fresh, fruity scent with a hint of sweet spice. Extracted by cold expression of the peel of the under-ripe fruit. Bergamot contains furocoumarins (notably bergapten) which are phototoxic and cause sensitization and skin pigmentation when exposed to direct sunlight. Always use bergapten free oil (otherwise known as FCF, furocoumarin free).

black pepper (*Piper nigrum*) Extracted by steam distillution of the dried and crushed peppercorns, this oil has a very dry, woody, spicy scent. An irritant in large doses, but a couple of drops are all you need to spice up your blend before the peppery scent becomes too dominant.

carnation (*Dianthus caryophyllus*) A lingering, rich, honey-like scent with a hint of spicy cloves. Extracted from the fresh flowers of this low-growing perennial. A lovely perfume just on its own and reported to be an aphrodisiac, but a very expensive oil.

chamomile, German (*Matricaria recutica*) A strong, sweet, herbaceous odor. Steam distillation of the flower heads produces a thick, inky blue oil.

chamomile, Roman (*Anthemis nobilis*) A very relaxing oil with a fruity-sweet, herbaceous scent. Similar to German chamomile without the blue color.

cinnamon leaf (*Cinnamomum zeylanicum*) A warm, spicy, slightly harsh odor, extracted from the leaves and twigs of this tropical tree. Always use leaf oil rather than bark oil, although even cinnamon leaf can be a skin irritant if used in large quantities. Add carefully and at a light trace as it may also make your soap seize.

clary sage (*Salvia sclarea*) Closely related to the garden sage and highly esteemed during the Middle Ages, clary sage has a sweet, nutty, slightly dominating herbaceous scent. It is a soothing oil, good for inflamed skin but do not use while drinking alcohol as it can exaggerate the feeling of drunkenness.

clove bud (*Syzygium aromaticum*) A sweet and spicy liquid with a fruity-fresh top note. Produced by distillation of the dried calyx of the slender, evergreen tree. Can cause mucus membrane and skin irritation. Always use clove bud, not clove leaf, oil. Only use in very tiny amounts (less than 1%) in your recipe. A little goes a long way – this is a penetrating oil, very slow to fade.

eucalyptus, blue gum (*Eucalyptus globulus*) A thin, clear liquid with a distinctive camphoric odor. Distilled from the leaves and young twigs. A useful, medicated oil with strong antiseptic properties, good for greasy skins. Do not take internally as even a tiny dose of a couple of millilitres has proved fatal.

eucalyptus, lemon (*Eucalyptus citriodora*) Similar to eucalyptus blue gum, but with a strong, citronella, lemony-like scent. This oil is highly toxic.

frankincense (*Boswellia thurifera*) Warm, rich, and sweet. A wonderful oil and a must for festive recipes. Frankincense is derived from a gum, collected by making incisions into the bark of the tree.

gardenia (*Gardenia jasminoides*) Buttery rich, floral, and jasmine-like. A dark, oily liquid obtained by solvent extraction from the fresh flowers. A lot of gardenia oil is now synthetically produced, so check before you buy.

geranium (*Pelargonium graveolens*) A greenish-olive liquid with a rosy delicate scent extracted from the leaves, stalks, and flowers of the rose geranium plant. A very feminine oil that combines well with most other floral, citrus, and spice oils.

ginger (*Zingiber officinale*) A warm, woody, spicy scent with a slightly green note, extracted from the dried, ground roots. A very warming oil, good for muscular aches and pains.

grapefruit (*Citrus x paradisi*) A greenish liquid with a fresh, tangy, citrus scent. Extracted by cold expression of the fresh peel. Fades quickly when added to soaps unless combined with deeper notes to anchor it. However, the scent does last better when added to liquid soap preparations. Like all citrus oils, it can oxidize quickly.

helichrysum (*Helichrysum angustifolium*) Also known as Immortelle. Distilled from the fresh flowers to produce a rich, sweet, honey scent with a delicate tea-like undertone.

honeysuckle (*Lonicera caprifolium*) Creamy-sweet with a fresh, floral, spicy note. A beautiful but expensive oil. Use in conjunction with honeysuckle floral water to make the cost less prohibitive.

hop (*Humulus lupulus*) As well as being a major ingredient for beer, hops are also a traditional remedy for insomnia. Distilled from the catkins, called strobiles, hop oil has a rich, spicy-sweet aroma that blends well with citrus and spice oils.

jasmine (*Jasminum officinale*) An evergreen vine with delicate, star-shaped, highly fragrant flowers. An intensely rich and sweet oriental, floral fragrance.

juniper berry (*Juniperus communis*) Juniper berries are a major flavor ingredient in gin. The essential oil has a clear, crisp, slightly woody scent. Should not be used by anyone suffering from kidney disease or during pregnancy.

lavender, true (*Lavandula angustifolia*) Sweet, floral, herbaceous, woody. An unmistakable scent and an eternal favorite. Distilled from the fresh flowering tops, this is also a very relaxing, cooling, and healing oil.

lavender, spike (*Lavandula latifolia*) Similar to true lavender but with a more penetrating, camphoric, herbaceous aroma.

lemon (*Citrus limon*) Cold expression of the fresh peel produces this light, fresh, citrus scent. Do not use on skin exposed to direct sunlight as this oil is phototoxic.

lemongrass (*Cymbopogon citratus*) A fast growing, perennial grass that, when finely chopped and distilled, produces a fresh, grassy, lemony scent. Use with caution as it can cause skin irritation.

lime (*Citrus aurantifolia*) A fresh, sharp, fruity citrus scent. More penetrating and less prone to fading in soaps than other citrus oils.

litsea cubeba (*Litsea cubeba*) A small tropical tree with lemongrass-scented leaves and flowers, the fruits of which are distilled to produce an oil with a fresh, fruity, sherbet-lemon odor.

mandarin (*Citrus reticulata*) The lightest and most delicate of all the citrus oils with an intensely sweet, almost floral-like scent.

marjoram, sweet (*Origanum majorana*) Steam distilled from the flowering herb to produce a warm, woody, slightly camphoric oil. Avoid during pregnancy.

mimosa (*Acacia dealbata*) A dark, viscous liquid with a deep, woody, floral, slightly green scent. Acts as a good fixative to other oils.

myrrh (*Commiphora myrrha*) A mellow, slightly spicy, balsamic odor. Extracted in a similar way to frankincense. The two oils go hand in hand and have a history of over 4000 years of use.

myrtle (*Myrtus communis*) A pale yellow oil distilled from the leaves and twigs of this fragrant bush. The scent is somewhat similar to that of eucalyptus, being clear, fresh, camphoric, and sweet.

neroli (*Citrus aurantium*) Steam distilled from the freshly picked flowers of the bitter orange tree. A light, sweet, intensely floral fragrance with a slight terpeney top note. Traditionally used in eau-de-cologne and toilet waters.

nutmeg (*Myristica fragrans*) An aromatic spice oil with a warm, balsamic fragrance. Like most spice oils, it has a strong, dominant, lingering scent that acts as a good fixative in soaps. Use in moderation and with care in pregnancy.

oakmoss (*Evernia prunastri*) Very viscous and dark greeny brown in color. Oakmoss acts as an excellent fixative and blends well with most other oils. The tenacious, earthy-mossy absolute is extracted from a lichen found growing on oak trees.

orange, bitter (*Citrus aurantium* var. *amara*) An evergreen citrus tree, the fruits of which are smaller and darker than the sweet orange. The oil has a dry, almost floral scent and is extracted, like other citrus oils, by cold expression from the peel of the fruit.

orange, sweet (*Citrus sinensis*) Similar to bitter orange but with a sweeter, fruity fragrance.

palmarosa (*Cymbopogon martinii*) A wild growing grass in the same family as lemongrass but with a sweet, floral, rosy, geranium type scent. Moisturizes and stimulates cellular regeneration, so very effective in skin applications. Blends well with rose and geranium and other floral oils.

patchouli (*Pogostemon cablin*) A viscous, amber oil that is beneficial to dry and cracked skin. Used traditionally to scent linens due to its rich, sweet, earthy aroma.

peppermint (*Mentha piperita*) A perennial garden herb with a distinctive, grassy, minty, camphoric scent. Not to be confused with corn mint (*Mentha arvensis*). There are many different types of mint but Mitcham mint is considered of superior quality. A cooling, stimulating oil where a little goes a long way.

petitgrain (*Citrus aurantium*) Steam distilled from the leaves and twigs of the bitter orange tree. At one time the oil used to be extracted from the unripe green oranges when they were still the size of a cherry, hence its name, petitgrains, or little grains. With its woody, herbaceous, citrus scent it is the third distinct oil produced from the same plant and one of the classic ingredients of eau-de-cologne.

pine (*Pinus sylvestris*) An essential oil distilled from the needles of the Scotch pine. The scent is strong, dry, and disinfectant-like so it will add a clean, medicated feel to your blends.

rosemary (*Rosmarinus officinalis*)
A sacred plant and one of the earliest to be used for food, medicine, and magic. The scent is fresh, minty, herbaceous, and balsamic. Poorer quality oils have a strong camphoric note. Not to be used during pregnancy or by epileptics.

rose otto and maroc (*Rosa damascena* and *Rosa centifolia*) Roses are traditionally associated with Venus, the goddess of love and beauty. The scent is deep, sweet, and tenacious with a rosy-spicy, honey-like note. Only a couple of species are used to produce the oil and an enormous amount of petals are needed to produce just a tiny amount of oil, which accounts for the high price of this most delightful ingredient.

sandalwood (*Santalum album*) One of the oldest known perfume materials with a history going back over 4000 years. The oil is extracted from the heartwood of thirty-year-old trees, producing a sticky, yellowish liquid with a deep, soft, beautiful, woody scent.

tea tree (*Melaleuca alternifolia*) Anti-fungal, anti-viral and anti-bacterial, tea tree is a powerful and healing natural antiseptic. Excellent for teenage skins and cleaning hands after a day in the garden. The scent is clear, medicated, and slightly camphoric, so is much more appealing in a blend. On its own it can be a little drying on the skin too, so, if your skin is not oily, this is best counteracted by mixing with more moisturizing oils.

thyme, lemon (*Thymus citriodorus*) The name thyme is derived from the ancient Greek *thymos*, meaning to perfume. There are various types of thyme oil, each distilled from a different variety, and not all are suitable for skin applications. Lemon thyme has a fresh, herbaceous, lemon scented aroma.

tuberose (*Polianthes tuberosa*) Expensive, but heavenly, with a heavy, sweet, tenacious scent. The plant itself is fairly easy to grow, with long, slender leaves and very fragrant, lily-like flowers so, if you feel the oil is too expensive for your budget, you could grow your own.

valerian root (*Valeriana officinalis*) A warm, woody, musky scented oil, distilled from the rhizomes of this native European perennial. Valerian is a highly relaxing oil that adds a mossy feel to your scent blends.

vanilla (*Vanilla planifolia*) The creamy, sweet scent is easily recognizable. The plant itself grows as a tall vine with large, trumpet-shaped white flowers. In their natural habitat, the flowers are pollinated by hummingbirds, and some eight or nine months later the pods are then harvested. The pods then have to be dried and cured for a further six months before the vanilla oil can be extracted.

vetivert (*Vetiveria zizanoides*) A tufted perennial grass with an abundant lacework of underground white rootlets. It is from these roots that the essential oil is produced. A dark brown, viscous liquid with a deep, smoky, woody, earthy aroma. A highly relaxing oil and a good fixative in soaps.

violet leaf (*Viola odorata*) A high-class perfume extracted from the freshly picked leaves. A dark green, viscous liquid with a delicate, floral, green-leaf scent.

ylang ylang (*Cananga odorata*) A tall tropical tree with fragrant yellow, pink, or mauve flowers. The yellow flowers are considered to produce the best essential oil. Intensely sweet with a creamy, soft, balsamic scent, ylang ylang is renowned for its aphrodisiac qualities, though in excessive concentrations it can cause headaches! Typically the flowers are distilled four times. The first, and superior, oil is called ylang ylang extra. The three successive distillates are called grades 1, 2, and 3 respectively and each of these grades has its own distinctive characteristics.

---

warning
Essential oils are powerful, pure and natural ingredients. If you have any sensitivity, are pregnant, epileptic, or suffer from high or low blood pressure, please consult your medical practitioner before use. Do not allow direct skin contact with undiluted essential oils. Keep away from children and pets and never take any essential oils internally. Always keep essential oils in well-labeled dark glass bottles and store in a cool, dark place.

basic techniques

cold processed soaps

Of all the techniques described in this book, cold processed soap making is probably the most complicated and most time consuming. But don't be put off – this soap will be far superior to anything you've ever tried before. It is gentle and moisturizing, so won't leave your skin feeling dry. That it is made solely from natural ingredients is a reassuring bonus in these days of mass production.

See the Warning on page 27 before you start. Sodium hydroxide dissolved in water is called lye. Your lye mixture will get very hot, very quickly and give off some noxious fumes, so work in a well-ventilated place.

1 Weigh all your base oils and then place in a large stainless steel saucepan. Weigh the water and pour into a large, heatproof cup or jug. Prepare your essential oils and botanicals and set them to one side. Accuracy with all your measurements is of prime importance to avoid making a soap that is either too soft or too harsh to use.

2 Wearing goggles, gloves, a face mask, and a protective apron, slowly and carefully pour the measured amount of sodium hydroxide into the water and stir until the granules are fully dissolved. Never pour the water into the sodium hydroxide. Take care not to splash the liquid as you pour.

3 Next, coordinate the temperatures of the base oils and lye solution. The lye must cool to around 122–140°F (50–60°C) in a well-ventilated place. Place the saucepan of base oils over a gentle heat to around 167–185°F (75–85°C). Remove from the heat.

4 Carefully pour the cooled lye solution into your pan of warmed base oils, stirring all the time with a slotted plastic or stainless steel spoon.

5 The solution will probably initially try to separate with the oils rising to the surface. Keep stirring and mixing to reincorporate the mixture. Stir continuously and the mixture will gradually thicken. Depending on your recipe, the base oils used, and the temperature of your mixture, this process may take a few minutes or even a few hours.

6 To find out if your soap is ready to pour into the mold, drag a spoon across the surface of the mixture. When a visible trail (known as a trace) is left behind that lasts for at least a few seconds, the mixture is ready to pour into the mold.

7 Once your soap mixture has traced, stir in the essential oils and any botanicals you wish to use, and pour into your mold.

8 Wrap the mold in a layer of blankets or old towels, and leave it to set for 24–48 hours. The blankets act as an insulating layer and stop the heat from the soap mixture escaping. This is called the gel stage.

9 Once your soap is completely cool, turn it out of the mold. Your soap block will be too soft and a little too harsh to use straight away and will need to mature, or cure, for approximately 4–6 weeks. Leave your soap somewhere cool and dark and try to forget about it. Your patience will be rewarded as, over the next few weeks, your soap will harden and mellow. You can then cut it into slices with a sharp knife and use as you wish.

liquid soaps

Traditionally, liquid soaps are made from potassium hydroxide rather than sodium hydroxide. However, there is a very acceptable alternative. It is very quick and easy to make, allows you to use up leftover chunks of soap that are otherwise too small but too good to throw away, and has the advantage of enabling you to include certain essential oils and floral waters that would fade too quickly in the cold processed soap method. An optional teaspoonful (5 ml) each of glycerine and vodka, added along with the essential oils, will improve the texture and add extra skin softening properties to your liquid soap.

1 Finely grate some leftover chunks of soap or use readymade clear soap base pellets or soap base block, easily available from specialist suppliers (see page 125). If using a soap base block, grate it first.

2 Add the grated soap to the top of your double boiler, mix in the water, and slowly melt over a medium heat.

3 When fully melted, remove the pan from the heat, stand aside for a few minutes to cool, then add your essential oils and mix well.

4 If you wish, you can further adjust the consistency of your liquid soap by adding more water. Floral waters are perfect for diluting, as they add their own delicate scent. Store your liquid soap in an airtight container to avoid further evaporation and thickening.

clear soaps

Making clear soap is very easy. Simply melt some clear soap base, easily obtainable from specialist suppliers (see page 125), add your chosen essential oils and botanicals, and pour into molds. Clear soap base is available as pellets or in a solid block. A solid block of clear soap base is easier to melt if grated first.

With a little supervision, older children will find the clear soap technique easy to master and produce some wonderful results. This form of soap making also has the advantage that it does not require any curing time, so the soap produced is ready to use straight away.

1 Fill the bottom half of a double boiler with water and put on to heat. In the meantime, weigh out the soap granules and prepare your essential oils and botanicals.

2 When the water is boiling, turn the heat down to simmering point and add the granules to the top half of the double boiler. Leave to melt, stirring occasionally.

3 When fully melted, remove from the heat and set aside to cool for a couple of minutes. If any scum has formed on the surface of the soap, simply scoop off and discard. Stir in the essential oils and botanicals.

4 Pour the soap into your mold. If the mixture is still quite warm, the botanicals will float to the top. If you would prefer them to be more evenly distributed, wait another minute or two for the soap to cool, then, just as the soap starts to thicken, stir again.

5 Your soap will cool and set hard in just an hour or two. It can then be popped out of the mold and cut into bars using a sharp knife. Your soap is now ready to use.

bath bombes

This is another recipe that children can easily master. Bath bombes are very simple and quick to make, and are popular presents. They are great for softening your bath water too, and leave your skin feeling soft and smooth. Use an oil mister (available from kitchen shops) for spraying on essential oils and a hollow, round mold divided into halves.

1 In a large mixing bowl, sieve together the sodium bicarbonate, citric acid, and cornstarch. Mix together well.

2 Slowly spray on the essential oils thinly and evenly, using an oil mister. Spray only a few drops at a time and mix in well as you go. You need less essential oil than you think. The mixture is ready when it just about holds together when pressed firmly between your fingers.

3 Divide the mixture into two equal portions and color with herbs, spices, and flower petals.

4 Pack the mixture firmly into your mold. Press the two halves together and clip together.

5 Set aside for 4–5 hours (or preferably overnight) to fully harden, then remove from the mold with a firm, twisting action. Leave your bombes to fully dry and harden for another day and they are ready to use.

massage melts

With massage melts you need never suffer from dry skin again. A massage melt is a solid bar that softens with the gentle warmth of your hands, so you can apply thick, luxurious oils just where your skin needs them most.

1 Get everything you need ready before you start. Weigh out your ingredients and set them aside in separate dishes.

2 Melt your base oils in a pan over a gentle heat. Melt the harder ingredients, such as cocoa butter and beeswax, first, then add the lighter oils, such as sweet almond, and warm through.

3 When fully melted, remove from the heat and stand aside for a couple of minutes to cool. Add the essential oils and stir in. Carefully pour the mixture into your molds.

4 Set aside for a couple of hours to cool and set. When soft set, transfer the melts to the fridge until they are really hard. They should then pop easily out of the molds. Decorate with dried flowers or herbs of your choice.

creating recipes

Once you have mastered the soap recipes in this book, why not design your own? Start by deciding what qualities you want your soap to have then design your recipe with proportions of base oils to suit – see the descriptions of base oils on pages 12–13 to help you decide. Olive makes a very hard bar with a silky lather. Coconut oil is the one to use if you want big bubbles, and palm oil produces a long-lasting bar and speeds up trace times. For a hard bar with a good lather, it is a good idea to include a large proportion of olive and coconut oil in your recipe.

When making up a recipe of your own it is crucial that you are very accurate with your measurements. In soap-making terms, making even a couple of pounds (a kilo) of soap is quite a small batch. An ounce or gram or two of inaccuracy can make the difference between success and failure, so make sure that your scales are accurate.

   The amount of sodium hydroxide you need to turn a specific amount of oil into soap varies according to base oil variety. This is called the oil's saponification value. Once you know the saponification value for each oil, it is then just a case of simple arithmetic to calculate the amount of sodium hydroxide needed. The saponification values for the base oils used in the recipes are given in the chart, right.

   Use the formula, above right, to calculate how much sodium hydroxide and water you require. Multiply the amount of oil you are using (in ounces or grams) by the oil's saponification value to give you the amount of sodium hydroxide needed (in ounces or grams). If you are using more than one base oil in your recipe, calculate them separately then add them together. For a creamy, moisturizing bar, it is best to leave a proportion of the oils in your recipe unsaponified. A 5% discount is a good figure to work with, giving a balance between a bar that still cleans effectively but also moisturizes without leaving your skin feeling greasy.

basic formula – sodium hydroxide

(base oil x sap value) x 95% = amount of sodium hydroxide needed

basic formula – water

To calculate the amount of water your recipe will need, multiply the weight of base oils by 0.375.
base oil x 0.375 = amount of water needed, by weight.

example

1 To make just over 2 lb (1 kg) of soap, decide your percentage breakdown of base oils, for example:
Imperial (50%) 1lb 1½ oz olive oil + (40%) 14 oz palm oil + (10%) 3½ oz rosehip oil
Metric (50%) 500 g olive oil + (40%) 400 g palm oil + (10%) 100 g rosehip oil

2 Use the saponification table to calculate the value for each oil and then calculate the weight of sodium hydroxide required:
Imperial ((1 lb 1½ oz x 0.134) + (14 oz x 0.141) + (3½ oz x 0.193)) x 95% = 4¾ oz
Metric ((500 x 0.134) + (400 x 0.141) + (100 x 0.193)) x 95% = 135 g

3 Calculate the amount of water required:
2 lb 2 oz x 0.375 = 13 oz
(1000 g x 0.375 = 375g)

saponification values

These figures are approximate. Various factors dictate the saponification value of each oil and often the saponification figure covers a range of values. Always check the saponification value of the oils you intend to use with your supplier.

avocado .133	palm, yellow and
beeswax .069	white .141
borage .136	pumpkin .135
castor .128	rosehip .193
cocoa butter .137	shea butter .128
coconut .190	sunflower .134
jojoba .069	sweet almond .136
olive .134	walnut .136
	wheatgerm .132

tips and tricks

Carefully follow the step-by-step guidelines on pages 20–25, and your recipes should be a success. The tips and common sense advice offered below will also help things to run smoothly.

• Get everything ready first and set out in the order that you need it. Weigh out your base oils, have your herbs in a bowl to one side, and measure out your essential oils. Read through the recipe and familiarize yourself with what you need to do. Once the soap-making process begins, you will need to have everything to hand to enable you to work quickly.

• Safety must come first. Until it has been turned into soap, sodium hydroxide is highly caustic and can cause serious burns, so treat it with respect. Always wear goggles, gloves, face mask, and protective apron when making cold processed soap.

• Work in a well-ventilated place – sodium hydroxide gets very hot and gives off some very noxious fumes when mixed with water.

• Protect all work surfaces with newspaper or plastic sheeting. Both sodium hydroxide and certain essential oils will irreparably mark and damage your work tops.

• Work in a controlled and methodical manner to avoid accidents or mistakes.

• Cleanliness and hygiene are essential.

• Do not allow pets or children into your work area while making cold processed soaps. (However, bombes, melts, and clear soap recipes are safe for children to make under supervision.)

• Keep thorough records and methodically write up everything you do. If you create a masterpiece, you'll want to be able to do it again.

• Record the batch numbers of all your ingredients and make sure that they are well within their use by date. If your ingredients aren't fresh, don't expect good results.

• Accuracy when measuring is very important. A dash of this and a splash of that just won't work.

• Make sure that the containers you use are large enough. You want to be able to stir your mixture without the risk of spillages.

• Although most of the equipment you will need to make soap can be found in your kitchen, it is wise to keep a dedicated set of soap making utensils. Don't be tempted to use them for food again afterward.

warning
Sodium hydroxide is very dangerous. It is a strong alkali and can cause serious burns. Do not take internally as it is highly poisonous. If it comes into contact with the skin, wash immediately and thoroughly in plenty of running water. Vinegar may help to neutralize its effect. If it comes in contact with your eyes, rinse with copious amounts of water and seek medical advice. Keep away from children and pets, and keep in the original, well-labeled container.

Essential oils are powerful, pure, and natural ingredients which, when used correctly, have many beneficial effects. However, if you have any sensitivity, are pregnant, epileptic, or suffer from high or low blood pressure, please consult your medical practitioner before use. Do not allow direct skin contact with undiluted essential oils. Keep away from children and pets and never take any essential oils internally. Always keep essential oils in well-labeled dark glass bottles and store in a cool, dark place.

troubleshooting

So things didn't go quite as planned. What went wrong? It is always helpful to know why a recipe didn't quite work out, so that you can improve it and be successful the next time.

There may be many different reasons why your recipe didn't work. The check list below gives some solutions to the most commonly occurring problems.

cold processed soap

My soap mixture has suddenly separated into a semi-transparent goo and looks like lumpy scrambled eggs.
Your soap mixture has seized. This is usually caused by mixing your base oils and lye at too high a temperature. Some essential oils can also cause seizing, notably cinnamon, clove, and myrrh. If you can act quickly and pour the soap mixture into your mold, you may be able to save the batch.

There is a white powdery film on top of my soap.
This film is called soap ash. Although it is not aesthetically pleasing, it is quite harmless and can easily be washed or sliced off. To avoid the powder forming, cover your molds as soon as you have poured in the soap mixture and do not let it set at too low a temperature.

I've made my soap but it won't harden properly and still feels soft.
When first removed from the mold, your soap will probably still be a little soft. Leave it for a few weeks to air-dry and harden before use. If it remains soft, it may have been caused either by the soap setting at too low a temperature or by measuring your ingredients incorrectly in the first place. If this is the cause, your soap will still be mild enough to use but may leave your skin feeling a little greasy.

There is a thick layer of oil on top of my set soap.
You may have poured your soap into the mold before it had fully traced. The rest of the soap will almost certainly be too harsh to use – throw it away and put it down to experience.

My soap is brittle and crumbly.
There are two possible causes. The first, and less serious reason, is that you have added too little water, the other is that you have measured incorrectly and added too much sodium hydroxide (or too little oils). Test to make sure that your soap is not too harsh. If the latter is the problem, you can turn it into liquid soap if you mix it with much milder soap.

liquid soap

My liquid soap is a little lumpy.
This is simply a case of not mixing your grated soap and liquid together properly. Remelt your liquid soap and stir until it is of a smooth, even consistency. For your next recipe, grate the soap a little finer.

clear soap

A little bit of scum always seems to form on the top of my melted soap. What am I doing wrong?
This is quite common and all you need to do is to let your soap mix cool for a couple of minutes then scoop it from the surface. Dust and dirt on your equipment, or in your water or herbs, may all contribute to scum, so make sure that everything is sparklingly clean before you start.

There are tiny air bubbles in my finished soap bars.
This is caused by pouring your soap into the mold too

quickly. Sometimes it can add a pleasing aesthetic touch to your soaps, like dew on early morning flower petals, but mostly it is an unwelcome feature, so pour your soap slowly and carefully and try to avoid trapping air in with the mixture.

My finished soap looks a little cloudy.
You've probably got a little bit of water from your double boiler in with your base soap. This is not the end of the world and provided you've not added too much, it won't adversely affect your finished soap. In some cases it can even look quite attractive.

I can see crystallized lumps in my soap.
You stirred your soap mix just as it was on the point of setting. Once poured into the mold, don't touch your soap mix unless you have to.

Why do the botanicals I add to my soap always float to the top instead of being evenly distributed throughout the bar?
You've added your botanicals while the soap mix is still too hot. Let it cool for a few minutes before stirring in your herbs or flower petals. If they still try to float to the top, let the soap mix cool for another couple of minutes, then stir again.

bath bombes

My bombes are growing out of the molds!
You've probably added too much moisture to your mixture – you really do need less than you think.

Ambient temperature also plays a part. Sodium bicarbonate is a raising agent, so too high a room temperature will also start the mixture rising.

My bath bombes are cracking as they dry out.
Your sodium bicarbonate and/or citric acid is possibly too coarse a grade. Both powders should be a very fine consistency, similar to icing sugar. They are easy to grind down to a finer powder, so the problem is quickly rectified. If your bombes are cracking along the join of the mold, then you haven't packed the mixture tightly enough. Cracked bombes will fizz just as well so don't throw them away, just save them for your own use rather than giving them as presents.

Where did all the fizz go?
Citric acid and sodium bicarbonate react together with water to form carbon dioxide and that's what you see as the fizz. If your fizz has gone flat, check first that your ingredients were fresh and dry before you started. If they were, did you add too much liquid when mixing, starting the fizz reaction, or have you stored your finished bombes somewhere damp?

massage melts

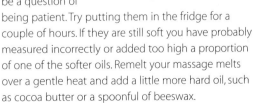

My melts are still soft and don't seem to be setting …
It may well just be a question of being patient. Try putting them in the fridge for a couple of hours. If they are still soft you have probably measured incorrectly or added too high a proportion of one of the softer oils. Remelt your massage melts over a gentle heat and add a little more hard oil, such as cocoa butter or a spoonful of beeswax.

… likewise if you are finding them too hard to use.
Remelt and add a little more soft oil, such as sweet almond or shea butter.

the recipes

floral

passion flower melts

Rich, thick, and creamy massage melts with the alluring perfume of ylang ylang, vetivert, and tuberose, enveloping a penetrating blend of shea butter, jojoba, and sweet almond oil.

ingredients

3½ oz/100 g shea butter

3½ oz/100 g white beeswax

2 oz/50 g jojoba oil

2 oz/50 g sweet almond oil

½ tsp/2.5 ml ylang ylang essential oil

½ tsp/2.5 ml vetivert essential oil

30 drops tuberose essential oil

dried red roses

1 Follow the detailed step-by-step instructions on page 25. Place the shea butter, beeswax, jojoba, and almond oils in a small saucepan and melt slowly over a low heat.

2 When fully melted, remove from the heat and stand aside for a couple of minutes to cool a little. Stir in the essential oils.

3 Carefully pour the mixture into heart-shaped molds and leave to set for a couple of hours.

4 Once set, the finished melts should easily pop out of the molds. If not, place them carefully in the fridge, leave them for half an hour or so and try again.

5 Decorate the top of each melt with a single dried red rose.

white lavender

Castile soap has been cherished for centuries for its gentle, silky lather. Made with pure olive oil and nothing else, this simple soap is infused with English lavender essential oil.

ingredients

4½ oz/130 g sodium hydroxide

13 oz/375 g spring water

2 lb 2 oz/1 kg olive oil

4 tsp/20 ml English lavender essential oil

1 Follow the detailed step-by-step instructions on pages 20–21. In a well-ventilated place, carefully add the sodium hydroxide to the spring water and stir gently until fully dissolved. Set aside to cool.

2 Gently warm the olive oil over a low heat in a stainless steel saucepan. Remove the oil from the heat and carefully stir in the lye using a slotted spoon.

3 Continue stirring until the mixture thickens and traces. Olive oil is renowned for taking a long time to trace, so this process may take a few hours. Insulating your pan with slabs of polystyrene or wrapping the outside in a blanket may help reduce trace times.

4 When your mixture has traced, add the lavender essential oil and stir in. Pour the soap mixture into your mold. An attractive jelly mold works well and adds fine detailing to an otherwise simple soap.

5 Cover your mold with blankets and set aside for 24–48 hours to cool. Turn out of the mold and leave somewhere cool and airy to mature for around 4–6 weeks before using.

sweet violets

With their vivid blue flowers and heart-shaped leaves, violets were the flower of Aphrodite, the goddess of love. A posy of sweetly-scented violets, disguised as a soap, makes a perfect gift.

ingredients

5 oz/145 g sodium hydroxide

13 oz/375 g spring water

1 lb 1½ oz/500 g olive oil

9 oz/250 g coconut oil

9 oz/250 g palm oil

2 tsp/10 ml violet leaf essential oil

2 tsp/10 ml geranium essential oil

1 tsp/5 ml alkanet

1 Follow the detailed step-by-step instructions on pages 20–21. In a well-ventilated place, carefully add the sodium hydroxide to the spring water. Stir gently until it is dissolved and set aside to cool.

2 Place the olive, coconut, and palm oils into a large stainless steel saucepan. Melt the base oils over a low heat and gently warm through.

3 Remove the pan from the heat and add the cooled lye solution. The oil will probably try to separate to the top, so gently stir to reincorporate the mixture.

4 Continue stirring with a slotted spoon until the mixture thickens and traces. Add the essential oils and stir in thoroughly.

5 Pour two thirds of the soap mixture into your molds then add the alkanet to the remaining mixture and stir in. Carefully spoon this remaining third over the soap mixture already in the mold.

6 Cover your mold with blankets and set aside for 24–48 hours to cool. Turn out of the mold and leave somewhere cool and airy for 4–6 weeks to harden and mature before use. You can then cut your soap into bar-sized slices using a sharp knife.

baby face

A simple soap with a delicate pink color, for the softest of skins and babies of all ages. The gentle, soothing action of borage oil is particularly suited to delicate young skin.

ingredients

4 tsp/20 ml ground rosehips

13 oz/375 g spring water

5 oz/145 g sodium hydroxide

1 lb 3 oz/600 g olive oil

10½ oz/300 g coconut oil

3½ oz/100 g borage oil

1 tsp/5 ml Roman chamomile essential oil

1 tbsp/15 ml mandarin essential oil

1 Tie the ground rosehips in a cheesecloth (muslin) bag and leave in the spring water to infuse for a couple of hours. Your spring water will turn a rich red color. Remove the bag.

2 Follow the detailed step-by-step instructions on pages 20–21. In a well-ventilated place, carefully add the sodium hydroxide to the infused spring water. Stir carefully until fully dissolved and leave to cool. Your solution will turn from a rich red into a dense, warm, rusty color.

3 Gently warm the base oils over a low heat in a stainless steel saucepan. Remove from the heat and carefully stir in the cooled lye solution.

4 Continue stirring with a slotted spoon to stop the oils separating. Your mixture will lighten in color and gradually thicken and trace. You may find that the addition of the rosehips will help reduce trace times, compared to some other recipes.

5 When traced thoroughly, stir in the essential oils and then pour your mixture into your mold.

6 Insulate your mold with blankets to help your soap mixture gel and leave covered for 24–48 hours until it has cooled. Turn out of the mold and leave somewhere cool and airy for around 4–6 weeks whilst your soap hardens and matures. Cut into bar sized chunks.

lavender and larkspur

A traditional, rustic soap, topped with a sprinkling of blue lavender buds and larkspur petals, combined with the scent of lavender fields in Provence.

ingredients

5¼ oz/150 g sodium hydroxide
13 oz/375 g spring water
14 oz/400 g olive oil
14 oz/400 g coconut oil
7 oz/200 g sweet almond oil
1 tbsp/15 ml French lavender essential oil
1 tsp/5 ml clary sage essential oil
lavender buds and larkspur petals

1 Follow the detailed step-by-step instructions on pages 20–21. In a well-ventilated place, carefully add the sodium hydroxide to the spring water. Stir gently until it is dissolved and set aside to cool.

2 Warm the olive, coconut and sweet almond oil in a stainless steel pan. Remove from the heat and pour in the cooled lye solution, stirring with a slotted spoon.

3 Continue stirring until your soap mix thickens and traces. Stir in the ground lavender buds and essential oils. Grind 2 tbsp/30 ml of the lavender buds and stir in. Ground lavender adds a delicate, earthy hue and fine texture to your soap. However, do not be tempted to use whole buds at this stage, as the petals separate and look like dead flies when mixed into a soap mixture!

4 Pour the soap mixture into your mold. Insulate well and leave to cool for 24–48 hours.

5 Turn the soap out of the mold. Your soap will still be quite soft at this stage. To complete the rustic look, press whole lavender and larkspur buds into one side of the soft soap. Wear gloves, as the soap will still be a little harsh.

6 Leave the finished soap block somewhere cool and airy to harden for 4–6 weeks before using.

rosehip and geranium

A delicate, feminine soap dotted with ground rosehips and rose geranium leaves, and enriched with moisturizing rosehip oil. The soft pink color will mellow and darken with time.

ingredients

4³⁄₄ oz/135 g sodium hydroxide

13 oz/375 g spring water

1 lb 1½ oz/500 g olive oil

14 oz/400 g palm oil

3½ oz/100 g rosehip oil

4 tsp/20 ml ground rosehips

4 tsp/20 ml ground rose geranium (*Pelargonium graveolens*) leaves

1 tbsp/15 ml geranium essential oil

40 drops rose otto essential oil

1 Follow the detailed step-by-step instructions on pages 20–21. In a well-ventilated place, carefully add the sodium hydroxide to the spring water and stir gently until fully dissolved. Set aside to cool.

2 Place the olive, palm, and rosehip oils into a large stainless steel pan and melt over a low heat. Remove from the heat and carefully stir in the cooled lye solution using a slotted spoon.

3 Continue stirring until the mixture thickens and traces. Stir in the ground rosehips and rose geranium leaves. Stir in the essential oils and mix in well.

4 Pour the soap mixture into your molds. Cover with blankets and set aside for 24–48 hours until completely cool.

5 Turn the cooled soap out of the molds and cut into bars, then leave your soap somewhere cool and airy for around 4–6 weeks to cure before using.

rose garland

Feminine, sensual, and seductive. Release a fizzing bouquet of roses into a warm, deep bath with these bath bombes. Relax and let the petals float around you.

ingredients

1 lb/450 g bicarbonate of soda

10½ oz/300 g citric acid

5 oz/145 g cornstarch

½ tsp/2.5 ml rose otto essential oil

1 tsp/5 ml rose water

1 tsp/5 ml paprika

dried rose buds

1 Follow the detailed step-by-step instructions on page 24. In a large mixing bowl, sieve together the bicarbonate of soda, citric acid, and cornstarch. Add the rose otto essential oil and rub in.

2 Slowly and evenly sprinkle on the rose water until the mixture just holds together when pressed firmly between your fingers.

3 Divide the mixture in half. Mix one half with paprika, leaving the other half plain white.

4 Pack alternate spoonfuls of white and pink mixture into spherical molds. Leave to harden for a couple of hours then turn out of the molds.

5 Decorate the top of the bombes with dried rose buds. Leave somewhere cool, dry, and airy to harden for a day or two before use.

midsummer night's dream

With a bouquet of daisies floating over the top and the aroma of geranium, lavender, myrtle, and rose, this soap evokes dreams of a warm, still summer's night.

ingredients

2 lb 2 oz/1 kg clear soap base

2 tsp/10 ml geranium essential oil

2 tsp/10 ml lavender essential oil

1 tsp/5 ml myrtle essential oil

40 drops rose essential oil

dried daisy flowers

1 Follow the detailed step-by-step instructions on page 23. Melt your clear soap base in the top half of a double boiler over a low heat. If you are using a solid soap base rather than granules, it is easier to work with if you grate it first.

2 When the base is fully melted, remove the pan from the heat and stand aside for a couple of minutes to start to cool. If any scum has formed on the surface of the soap base, carefully spoon it off.

3 Stir in the essential oils. Pour the soap mix into your molds and leave to cool slightly before carefully floating the daisies on top. Using a metal spoon, gently press down on the daisies so that they float just below the surface of the soap.

4 Leave your soap to cool and set. Don't be tempted to readjust the daisies once the soap has started to cool.

5 After a couple of hours your soap should pop easily out of the mold. It is ready to use and enjoy straight away.

jasmine and honeysuckle

The scents of a cottage garden on a sultry summer night are entwined in this liquid soap to create a soft, foaming liquid nectar.

ingredients

1 lb 1½ oz/500 g finely grated cold processed soap

1 cup/250 ml jasmine water

1 cup/250 ml honeysuckle water

½ tsp/2.5 ml jasmine essential oil

½ tsp/2.5 ml honeysuckle essential oil

1 tsp/5 ml lemon essential oil

1 Follow the detailed step-by-step instructions on page 22. Place the finely grated soap into the top half of a double boiler and stir in the jasmine and honeysuckle waters. Slowly melt over a low heat, stirring occasionally. You can add more or less floral water as you wish to adjust the consistency of your liquid soap.

2 Remove the pan from the heat and leave to cool for a couple of minutes. Stir in the essential oils.

3 Pour your liquid soap into attractive airtight bottles, allow to cool, and it is ready to use straight away.

sunflower and calendula

A bright, sunny, soothing soap infused with calendula petals and sunflower oil and the light, cheerful fragrance of bergamot, chamomile, and neroli.

ingredients

4½ oz/130 g sodium hydroxide

13 oz/375 g spring water

10½ oz/300 g olive oil

1 lb 1½ oz/500 g coconut oil

7 oz/200 g sunflower oil

2 tbsp/30 ml calendula petals

2 tsp/10 ml bergamot essential oil

1 tsp/5 ml Roman chamomile essential oil

1 tsp/5 ml neroli essential oil

1 Follow the detailed step-by-step instructions on pages 20–21. In a well-ventilated place, carefully add the sodium hydroxide to the spring water. Stir gently until it is dissolved and set aside to cool.

2 Place the olive, coconut, and sunflower oils into a large stainless steel pan and melt over a gentle heat. Remove from the heat and carefully stir in the cooled lye solution.

3 Continue stirring using a slotted spoon to prevent the mixture from separating. When the soap mixture has traced, stir in the calendula petals. To create a variety of textures you could grind some of the petals to a coarse powder with a pestle and mortar.

4 Stir in the essential oils and mix in well. Pour the soap mixture into your mold and sprinkle calendula petals on top.

5 Cover and insulate your mold with blankets and set aside for 24–48 hours until completely cool. Turn your soap out of the mold and leave somewhere cool and airy for 4–6 weeks to fully harden and mature. Your soap will then be ready to cut into bars and use.

elderflower
shower gel

A subtle hint of lemon adds a gentle sparkle to this cleansing cordial, evoking the fresh and delicate fragrance of early summer walks and country hedgerows.

ingredients

1 lb 1½ oz/500 g clear soap base pellets

2 cups/500 ml elderflower water

2 tsp/10 ml vodka

2 tsp/10 ml glycerine

2 tsp/10 ml lemon juice

2 tsp/10 ml lemon essential oil

1 Follow the detailed step-by-step instructions on page 22. Add the soap pellets to the top half of a double boiler, mix in the elderflower water, and slowly melt over a gentle heat. The clear mixture will turn to an opaque, snow white.

2 Remove from the heat and add the vodka, glycerine, lemon juice, and lemon essential oil. Stir well to combine all the ingredients.

3 Pour into airtight plastic dispenser bottles. Your shower gel is ready to use as soon as it is cool. As the mixture cools it will turn to a gel-like consistency. If you wish, you can adjust this by remelting and adding more elderflower water.

gardenia and clove bath salts

Exotic and enticing. Just a spoonful of scented salts will soften your bath water and fill the air with the rich, buttery, spicy scents of gardenia and clove.

ingredients

1 lb 1½ oz/500 g Epsom salts or coarse sea salt crystals

1 tsp/5 ml sweet almond oil

1 tsp/5 ml glycerine

40 drops gardenia essential oil

10 drops clove essential oil

40 drops rose maroc essential oil

rose petals and clove buds

1 Fill a bowl with Epsom salts or coarse sea salt crystals. Add the sweet almond oil, glycerine, and essential oils and stir well until evenly distributed.
2 Add the rose petals and clove buds and mix in.
3 Decant into attractive bottles and your salts are ready to use straight away.

citrus

limoncello

A clear, bright soap-on-a-rope evoking sun-soaked memories of the Amalfi coast, with the tangy fragrance of freshly squeezed lemons.

ingredients

2 lb 2 oz/1 kg clear soap base
2 tsp/10 ml yellow palm oil
1 tbsp/15 ml lemon essential oil
1 tsp/5 ml litsea cubeba essential oil
1 tsp/5 ml neroli essential oil
4 tsp/20 ml calendula petals
4 tsp/20 ml safflower petals
sea grass rope

1 Follow the detailed step-by-step instructions on page 23. Melt your clear soap base in the top half of a double boiler over a gentle heat. Add the yellow palm oil and stir until fully melted and mixed in with the soap base.

2 Remove from the heat and leave to cool for a couple of minutes. Stir in the essential oils, calendula, and safflower petals.

3 Pour into a round tube. A length of drainpipe, sealed at one end, makes an ideal mold.

4 After a couple of hours the soap will be fully hardened and should easily push out of your tube mold.

5 Cut into slices and make a hole in the center of each soap disc. An apple corer makes perfectly sized round holes. Thread sea grass rope through each disc to create a simple, natural looking soap-on-a-rope.

st clements

The scent of freshly squeezed lemons and the sweetness of mandarins combine to create a clean, bright, refreshing soap with a hint of the Mediterranean.

ingredients

5½ oz/155 g sodium hydroxide

13 oz/375 g spring water

10½ oz/300 g olive oil

1 lb 1½ oz/500 g coconut oil

3½ oz/100 g sweet almond oil

3½ oz/100 g yellow palm oil

2½ tsp/12.5 ml lemon essential oil

2½ tsp/12.5 ml mandarin essential oil

1 tsp/5 ml lemongrass

4 tsp/20 ml finely grated citrus peel

dried orange slices

1 Follow the detailed step-by-step instructions on pages 20–21. In a well-ventilated place, carefully pour the sodium hydroxide into the spring water. Stir gently until it is fully dissolved. Set aside to cool.
2 Melt the base oils together in a large stainless steel pan over a low heat. Remove from the heat and slowly and carefully add the lye, stirring gently all the time.
3 Continue stirring until the soap mixture thickens and traces. Add the essential oils and citrus peel and stir in.
4 Pour your soap mixture into your mold. Decorate the top with dried orange slices. Cover your mold with blankets so that the mixture gels then leave for 24–48 hours until it has completely cooled.
5 Remove the soap from the mold and leave somewhere cool and airy for about 4–6 weeks to harden and mature. Your soap is now ready to cut into slices and use.

For an attractive variation, top with lemon and lime slices.

lime wash

Wake up to this clean, bright shower soap. It has a sparkling aroma of freshly squeezed limes, with light and foaming bubbles to leave you feeling clean and refreshed. Perfect for cool showers on hot summer days.

ingredients

2 green tea bags

2 cups/500 ml spring water

1 lb 1.5 oz/500 g finely grated cold processed soap

1 tsp/5 ml yellow palm oil

2 tsp/10 ml lime essential oil

2 tsp/10 ml lime juice

1 Infuse the green tea in the spring water. When the desired color has been reached, remove the tea bags.

2 Follow the detailed step-by-step instructions on page 22. Place the finely grated soap into the top half of a double boiler and mix with the infused spring water. Melt over a low heat.

3 Stir until fully mixed and the melted soap is of an even consistency. Adjust the consistency of your liquid soap by altering the amount of liquid or grated soap you add.

4 Remove the double boiler from the heat and leave the mixture to cool for a couple of minutes before stirring in the essential oil and lime juice. Pour into airtight bottles and your soap is ready to use.

orange sherbet

Treat yourself to some fizz-o-therapy with this bubbly bath bombe packed full of effervescent orange scent.

ingredients

1 lb/450 g bicarbonate of soda

10.5 oz/300 g citric acid

5.25 oz/150 g cornstarch

½ tsp/2.5 ml litsea cubeba essential oil

1 tsp/5 ml bitter orange essential oil

1 tsp/5 ml turmeric powder

calendula petals

1 Follow the detailed step-by-step instructions on page 24. Sieve together the bicarbonate of soda, citric acid, and cornstarch.
2 Add the essential oils drop by drop and mix in well. Alternatively, use an oil mister to apply the essential oils thinly and evenly.
3 Mix in the turmeric powder. Stir in unevenly so that the mixture retains a marbled effect.
4 Place a couple of calendula petals in the bottom of each mold. Pack the two halves of the mold with the bombe mixture then place firmly together.
5 Hold the two halves together with clips and leave to dry for a few hours, or overnight if possible.
6 Using a twisting action, remove the bombes from the molds. They will be ready to use in a day or two, once they are fully dry.

marmalade

This clear, bright soap glistening with chunks of citrus peel has the zesty, tangy aroma of bitter oranges, mandarins, and limes with just a hint of ginger to add extra sparkle.

ingredients

2 lb 2 oz/1 kg clear soap base

1 tbsp/15 ml yellow palm oil

1 tsp/5 ml lime essential oil

2 tsp/10 ml mandarin essential oil

2 tsp/10 ml bitter orange essential oil

1 tsp/5 ml ginger essential oil

2 tbsp/30 ml grated citrus peel

1 Follow the detailed step-by-step instructions on page 23. Place your soap base into the top half of a double boiler and melt over a gentle heat.
2 Add the yellow palm oil and stir until fully melted and mixed in. Remove from the heat and stand aside for a minute or two to cool.
3 Stir in the essential oils and the grated citrus peel. A variety of different sized gratings will make your soap more interesting. Pour into the mold.
4 As the soap starts to cool and set, drag a spoon over the surface of the mixture to create a textured, jam-like topping.
5 Leave to cool and set for a couple of hours then pop out of the mold. Your soap is ready to cut into chunks and use straight away.

chocolate orange

A rich, dark, and luxurious soap cake, layered with lashings of organic chocolate, creamy cocoa butter, and sweet orange pure essential oil.

ingredients

5 oz/145 g sodium hydroxide

13 oz/375 g spring water

14 oz/400 g olive oil

10½ oz/300 g coconut oil

7 oz/200 g sweet almond oil

3½ oz/100 g yellow palm oil

2 tsp/10 ml bitter orange essential oil

2 tsp/10 ml sweet orange essential oil

2 tsp/10 ml mandarin essential oil

4 tsp/20 ml organic cocoa powder

dried orange slices

1 Follow the detailed step-by-step instructions on pages 20–21. In a well-ventilated place, carefully pour the sodium hydroxide into the spring water. Stir gently until it is fully dissolved. Set aside to cool.

2 Place the base oils in a large stainless steel pan and melt slowly over a gentle heat. Remove from the heat and carefully pour in the cooled lye solution.

3 Stir gently with a slotted spoon. Continue stirring and the mixture will gradually thicken and trace. Pour in the essential oils and stir well.

4 Divide the mixture in half and stir the cocoa powder into one portion. Make sure that your cocoa powder has a high cocoa butter content. Alternatively, choose a block of chocolate and grate very finely.

5 Pour the chocolate half into your molds first, then carefully spoon the remaining orange half on top. Decorate with a slice of dried orange.

6 Cover your molds with blankets and set aside for a couple of days to cool. Remove from the molds and place your soap cakes somewhere cool and airy to mature and harden. They will be ready to use in 4–6 weeks.

almond and orange blossom

A delicate, feminine fragrance with a hint of the exotic from the sensual, bittersweet contrast of bitter almonds and sweet orange blossom.

ingredients

1 lb 1½ oz/500 g finely grated cold processed soap

2 cups/500 ml orange flower water

2 tsp/10 ml vodka

2 tsp/10 ml glycerine

½ tsp/2.5 ml neroli essential oil

1 tsp/5 ml bitter almond oil

1 Follow the detailed step-by-step instructions on page 22. Place the finely grated soap into the top half of a double boiler. You could also add a little clear soap if you have some left over. Add the orange flower water and stir in thoroughly. Melt the soap over a low heat. You can adjust the consistency by adding more or less orange flower water.
2 Remove from the heat and stir in the vodka, glycerine, and essential oils.
3 Decant into pretty, airtight bottles and your liquid soap is ready to use as soon as it is cool.

citrus caramel

A thick, creamy massage melt with a light, buttery, citrus scent and the luscious melt-to-the-touch feel of shea butter.

ingredients

12 oz/350 g shea butter

3½ oz/100 g white beeswax

2 oz/50 g jojoba oil

15 drops benzoin essential oil

½ tsp/2.5 ml frankincense essential oil

1 tsp/5 ml sweet orange essential oil

¼ tsp/1.25 ml finely ground chocolate powder

¼ tsp/1.25 ml yellow palm oil

1 Follow the detailed step-by-step instructions on page 25. Melt the shea butter, beeswax, and jojoba oil together in a small pan over a gentle heat.

2 Remove the pan from the heat when the oils are fully melted and stand for a couple of minutes to allow the oils to cool. Stir in the essential oils and mix well.

3 Pour a couple of spoonfuls of the melt mixture into a separate bowl and mix with the chocolate powder. Place a spoonful of this mixture into the bottom of each mold. Crème caramel pots make an appropriate choice of mold.

4 Next, take out a few more spoonfuls of the melt mixture and place in a separate bowl. Stir in the yellow palm oil. Carefully spoon on top of the first layer in your molds.

5 Finally, top up the molds with the rest of the plain mixture. Allow to cool and set, then pop your melts out of the mold. All citrus oils are to some degree photo toxic, so avoid direct sunlight immediately after applying this massage melt.

lemon heaven

A zesty, cologne-scented bar filled with bergamot, neroli, and lemongrass. A moisturizing massage melt to refresh and nourish parched skin.

ingredients

12 oz/350 g cocoa butter

3½ oz/100 g shea butter

2 oz/50 g white beeswax

1 tsp/5 ml bergamot FCF essential oil

½ tsp/2.5 ml lemongrass essential oil

½ tsp/2.5 ml neroli essential oil

2 tsp/10 ml freshly squeezed lemon juice

2 tbsp/30 ml yellow palm oil

1 Follow the detailed step-by-step instructions on page 25. Place the cocoa butter, shea butter, and beeswax together in a small pan and melt over a low heat.

2 When fully melted, remove from the heat and stand aside for a minute or two to start to cool. Add the essential oils and lemon juice and stir in.

3 In a separate small pan, melt the yellow palm oil. This will not take long as you are only melting a very small quantity.

4 Swirl a spoonful of yellow palm oil into the bottom of each mold. Carefully pour on the rest of the melt mixture. Then leave your molds for a couple of hours to cool and set. Once they have soft set, you can place them in the fridge to fully harden.

5 Your melts should then slide easily out of the molds and are ready to use straight away.

mandarin moon

Round and round the mandarin moon. Soft round moons of sweet citrus scent encasing tiny flakes of citrus peel.

ingredients

5½ oz/155 g sodium hydroxide

13 oz/375 g spring water

12 oz/350 g olive oil

1 lb 3 oz/600 g coconut oil

2 oz/50 g jojoba oil

2 tsp/10 ml mandarin essential oil

2 tsp/10 ml bitter orange essential oil

2 tsp/10 ml bergamot FCF essential oil

4 tsp/20 ml grated citrus peel

1 Follow the detailed step-by-step instructions on pages 20–21. In a well-ventilated place, carefully add the sodium hydroxide to the spring water and stir gently until fully dissolved. Set aside to cool.

2 Gently melt the olive, coconut, and jojoba oils in a large stainless steel pan over a low heat. Remove from the heat and carefully pour in the cooled lye solution, stirring gently with a slotted spoon to stop the mixture from separating.

3 The mixture will gradually thicken and trace. Once the mixture has traced, add the essential oils and citrus peel and mix in thoroughly.

4 Pour into spherical molds then cover and insulate with blankets to retain the heat. Set aside for 24–48 hours to cool. Turn the cooled soap out of the mold. Leave your soap moons somewhere cool and airy for around 4–6 weeks before use. During this time they will mature and harden.

Round soaps fit snugly in the palms of your hands and so are easy to hold, making them an ideal shape for the elderly or young. They make an attractive variation to soap bars, too.

citrus sorbet

Swirls of creamy cocoa butter with a hint of citrus fruits and the sparkling aroma of grapefruit, orange, and lime. The light and fluffy lather will leave your skin feeling refreshingly clean.

ingredients

5¼ oz/150 g sodium hydroxide

13 oz/375 g spring water

10½ oz/300 g olive oil

1 lb 1½ oz/500 g coconut oil

7 oz/200 g castor oil

1 tbsp/15 ml grapefruit essential oil

2 tsp/10 ml lime essential oil

2 tsp/10 ml sweet orange essential oil

4 tsp/20 ml calendula petals

1 tsp/5 ml turmeric powder

curls of grated citrus peel

1 Follow the detailed step-by-step instructions on pages 20–21. In a well-ventilated place, carefully add the sodium hydroxide to the spring water and stir gently until fully dissolved. Set aside to cool.

2 Place the olive, coconut, and castor oils in a large stainless steel pan and melt over a low heat. Remove from the heat and carefully pour in the cooled lye solution. Stir with a slotted spoon to stop the oils separating and continue stirring until the mixture starts to thicken and trace.

3 Add the essential oils and calendula petals and stir thoroughly. Pour the soap mixture into your mold, then swirl in the turmeric powder to create a ripple effect. Top the mixture with curls of citrus peel.

4 Cover your soap mold with blankets to insulate and help the soap to gel, then leave for a couple of days until it has fully cooled.

5 Pop your soap out of the mold and leave somewhere cool and airy for 4–6 weeks to cure before cutting into bars and using.

honey and wheat germ

Sweet and sunny with a light, bright, lemony scent. Added flakes of wheat germ make this a gentle, naturally exfoliating soap to leave your skin feeling soft and smooth.

ingredients

5 oz/145 g sodium hydroxide

13 oz/375 g spring water

12 oz/350 g olive oil

14 oz/400 g coconut oil

7 oz/200 g sunflower oil

2 oz/50 g golden beeswax pellets

8 tsp/40 ml wheat germ

1 tbsp/15 ml lemon essential oil

2 tsp/10 ml lemongrass essential oil

1 tsp/5 ml organic honey

1 Follow the detailed step-by-step instructions on pages 20–21. In a well-ventilated place, carefully add the sodium hydroxide to the spring water and stir gently until fully dissolved. Set aside to cool.

2 Melt the base oils in a large stainless steel pan over a gentle heat. The beeswax will be the hardest to melt and if you have solid beeswax, rather than pellets, you may find it easier if you grate it first.

3 Remove the pan from the heat and carefully pour in the cooled lye solution, stirring all the time with a slotted spoon. Continue stirring and the mixture will gradually thicken and trace.

4 Add the wheat germ, essential oils, and honey and mix in well. Pour the soap mixture into your mold. Cover the mold with blankets to retain the heat and help the soap gel. Set aside for 24–48 hours to cool.

5 When your soap has fully cooled it is ready to turn out of the mold. Leave your soap block somewhere cool and airy for 4–6 weeks to harden and mature.

herbal

a hint of mint

A clear and minty liquid shower soap for cool and refreshing wake-me-up mornings. The peppermint oil will leave your skin feeling bright, tingly, and clean.

ingredients

1 lb 1½ oz/500 g finely grated cold processed soap

1 lb 1½ oz/500 g spring water

1 tsp/5 ml peppermint essential oil

1 Follow the detailed step-by-step instructions on page 22. Place the finely grated soap into the top half of a double boiler and add the spring water. Melt over a gentle heat and stir until the liquid soap is of an even consistency.

2 Remove the pan from the heat and leave to cool for a couple of minutes. Pour in the peppermint essential oil and mix well.

3 Your liquid soap is now ready to pour into airtight bottles and use. If you intend to use your soap as a shower soap, use sturdy plastic bottles rather than glass ones.

herbs and walnut

Walnut oil is a light, moisturizing oil that helps keep skin supple and smooth. Sprinkled with walnut leaves and calendula petals, this is a herbal soap with a sweet, green, woody scent.

ingredients

4½ oz/130 g sodium hydroxide

13 oz/375 g spring water

1 lb 5 oz/700 g pomace olive oil

5¼ oz/150 g castor oil

5¼ oz/150 g walnut oil

1½ tsp/7.5 ml sweet marjoram essential oil

½ tsp/2.5 ml petitgrain essential oil

½ tsp/2.5 ml rosemary essential oil

1½ tsp/7.5 ml valerian essential oil

2 tbsp/30 ml walnut leaves

2 tbsp/30 ml calendula petals

1 Follow the detailed step-by-step instructions on pages 20–21. Working in a well-ventilated place, pour the sodium hydroxide into the spring water. Stir until fully dissolved and leave to cool.

2 Place the pomace olive, castor, and walnut oils into a large stainless steel pan and melt over a low heat. Remove the pan from the heat and stir in the cooled lye solution.

3 Using a slotted spoon, keep stirring the soap mixture to stop the oils and lye separating. The mixture will gradually thicken and trace.

4 Add half of the walnut leaves and calendula petals together with the essential oils, and mix until evenly distributed throughout the soap.

5 Pour the soap into your mold then sprinkle crushed walnut leaves and calendula petals over the surface and press in lightly.

6 Cover and insulate your mold with old blankets and leave for a couple of days to cool completely. You can now turn your soap out of the mold and cut into bar-sized chunks. Leave to cure for 4–6 weeks before using.

herbal hair shine

A traditional herbal rinse for soft and shiny hair with a gentle lather and a clean, fresh scent.

ingredients

large handful of nettle leaves

large handful of rosemary sprigs

large handful of soapwort leaves

4 cups/1 ltr spring water

2 tsp/10 ml lemon juice

4 drops tea tree essential oil

4 drops lemon eucalyptus essential oil

4 drops rosemary essential oil

4 drops neroli essential oil

handful of soapwort flowers

1 Roughly chop the nettle, rosemary, and soapwort leaves and place in a large saucepan. Add the spring water, bring to the boil, cover, and simmer gently for 20 minutes.

2 Leave to cool, then strain. Coffee filter paper or a fine piece of cheesecloth (muslin) make ideal strainers. Stir in the lemon juice, essential oils, and soapwort flowers.

3 Leave the brew to infuse for about half an hour. Use as a final rinse when washing your hair, to leave it soft and shiny. Any leftover herbal infusion will keep for 24 hours if stored in the fridge.

parfum d'herbes
massage melt

A floral, green, herb-filled scent wrapped in a rich, buttery blend of cocoa butter and borage oil and topped with a sprig of scented sweet marjoram.

ingredients

1 lb/450 g cocoa butter

2 oz/50 g borage oil

10 drops clary sage essential oil

1 tsp/5 ml geranium essential oil

½ tsp/2.5 ml lime essential oil

sprigs of sweet marjoram

1 Follow the detailed step-by-step instructions on page 25. Slowly melt the cocoa butter and borage oil in a small pan. When fully melted, remove the pan from the heat and stand for a few minutes to cool.
2 Stir in the essential oils, then carefully pour the melt mixture into your molds. Small, individual yogurt pots make attractive molds that are just the right size to fit comfortably in your hand.
3 Leave your melt mixture to cool and set, then put in the fridge until really hard.
4 Your melts should now slide easily out of the molds. Top with a tiny sprig of sweet marjoram or other garden herb. Store in a cool place or, if the weather is warm, in the fridge.

sea herbs

Cool, fresh, and reviving like a breath of sea air. A clear, bright
wave of seaside herbs with a scrubby seaweed crust.

ingredients

2 lb 2 oz/1 kg clear soap base
pellets

1 tbsp/15 ml spike lavender
essential oil

½ tsp/2.5 ml peppermint
essential oil

1 tsp/5 ml rosemary essential
oil

1 tsp/5 ml powdered spirulina

a few grains of indigo powder

coarsely ground bladderwrack

1 Follow the detailed step-by-step instructions on
page 23. Melt the clear soap base in the top half of a
double boiler over a gentle heat.
2 When fully melted, remove from the heat and
leave to cool for a few minutes before stirring in the
essential oils.
3 Sprinkle on the spirulina and indigo powder and
stir in unevenly to create a marbled effect. You only
need the tiniest amount of powdered indigo as it
goes a long way. The spirulina will smell a little
unpleasant at first but don't worry; this will fade
rapidly leaving the benefit of its sea-green color and
the fresh aroma of the essential oils.
4 Pour the soap mixture into your molds. Allow to
cool for a further minute or two, then press the
crumbled bladderwrack seaweed into the surface of
the soap to create an attractive crusty topping.
5 As soon as the soap has cooled and hardened you
can pop it out of the mold and cut into bars with a
long, sharp knife. It is ready to use straight away.

beer soap

Hop flowers are known for their sedative qualities. Combined with lavender and mandarin and a glass of ale, this is a soap for long, lazy, relaxing baths.

ingredients

6 oz/175 g very, very flat beer
7 oz/200 g spring water
4½ oz/130 g sodium hydroxide
1 lb 1½ oz/500 g olive oil
7 oz/200 g cocoa butter
9 oz/250 g sweet almond oil
2 oz/50 g wheat germ oil
1 tsp/5 ml hop essential oil
2 tsp/10 ml lavender essential oil
1½ tsp/7.5 ml mandarin essential oil

1 Make sure that your beer is very, very flat before you start. Ideally, pour the beer into a wide-brimmed container, cover with a piece of cheesecloth (muslin), and leave to stand for at least two days before using.

2 Follow the detailed step-by-step instructions on pages 20–21. In a well-ventilated place, mix the flat beer with the spring water then slowly and carefully pour in the sodium hydroxide, stirring gently. At any sign of fizzing, stop immediately. If your beer is truly flat there should be no problem. Stir until the sodium hydroxide is completely dissolved and leave in a well-ventilated place to cool.

3 Melt the base oils in a large stainless steel pan over a low heat. Remove the pan from the heat and slowly pour in the cooled lye solution, stirring with a slotted spoon to stop the soap mixture from separating.

4 Continue stirring and after a while the mixture will gradually thicken and trace. Pour the soap into your mold, cover with a blanket, and leave for 24–48 hours for the soap to cool.

5 Remove from the mold. Your beer soap will be a lovely, creamy beige color. Cut into bars and leave somewhere cool and airy to harden and mature for around 4–6 weeks before use.

nettle and lavender

Country folklore says that nettles stimulate hair growth and help eliminate dandruff. This soap makes a good shampoo bar, keeping hair soft and shiny.

ingredients

large handful of freshly picked nettle leaves

13 oz/375 g spring water

5½ oz/155 g sodium hydroxide

1 lb 1½ oz/500 g coconut oil

14 oz/400 g olive oil

3½ oz/100 g castor oil

2½ tsp/12.5 ml lavender essential oil

2 tsp/10 ml tea tree essential oil

dried nettle leaves

1 Carefully wash the freshly picked nettle leaves and pat them dry. Place in a large mixing bowl and cover with boiling water. Leave the brew to infuse for about an hour then strain through a piece of fine cheesecloth (muslin) into a large heatproof cup or jug.

2 When the strained liquid has fully cooled, carefully pour in the sodium hydroxide and stir until dissolved. The reaction between the sodium hydroxide and liquid will reheat the liquid. Leave in a well-ventilated place to cool down again.

3 Melt the base oils in a large stainless steel pan over a low heat. Once fully melted, remove the pan from the heat and carefully pour in the nettle/lye solution. Stir with a slotted spoon to stop the soap mixture from separating.

4 The soap mixture will gradually thicken and trace. Stir in the essential oils and a handful of crumbled, dried nettle leaves.

5 Pour the soap mixture into your mold, insulate with a blanket and leave for 24–48 hours to set and cool. You can then remove your soap from the mold and cut into bars. Leave your soap somewhere cool and airy for 4–6 weeks to mature and harden.

rub scrub

A soap embedded loofa that will soften with water to gently exfoliate your skin. With a built-in sponge, this is a perfect idea for a travel soap.

ingredients

5¼ oz/150 g sodium hydroxide

13 oz/375 g spring water

10½ oz/300 g olive oil

14 oz/400 g coconut oil

9 oz/250 g sweet almond oil

2 oz/50 g shea butter

2 tsp/10 ml eucalyptus essential oil

1½ tsp/7.5 ml lavender essential oil

½ tsp/2.5 ml peppermint essential oil

1 tbsp/15 ml powdered parsley leaves

1 tbsp/15 ml powdered rosemary leaves

piece of loofa

1 Follow the detailed step-by-step instructions on pages 20–21. Working in a well-ventilated place, pour the sodium hydroxide into the spring water. Stir until completely dissolved then leave to cool.

2 Melt the olive oil, coconut oil, sweet almond oil, and shea butter together in a large stainless steel pan. Remove the pan from the heat and carefully pour in the cooled lye solution.

3 Stir with a slotted spoon until the mixture thickens and traces. This may take some time. Once the soap mixture has traced, stir in the essential oils and parsley and rosemary powder.

4 Place the loofa in a tall cylindrical mold and slowly pour the soap mixture over the loofa sponge. Tap the bottom of the mold to remove any trapped air bubbles then top up with more soap mixture. A section of drainpipe with a sealed end makes a good mold.

5 Cover the mold with blankets to insulate the soap so that it gels and leave for 24–48 hours to cool completely.

6 Slide the soap out of the mold and leave somewhere cool and airy for 4–6 weeks to harden and mature. You can then cut your loofa soap into slices. A serrated bread knife will cut smoothly and cleanly through the loofa.

herb garni

Use this bath bombe to infuse your bath water with a bubbling pot pourri of scented garden herbs and a sprinkling of flower petals.

ingredients

1 lb/450 g bicarbonate of soda

10½ oz/300 g citric acid

5¼ oz/150 g cornstarch

2 tsp/10 ml rosemary powder

30 drops basil essential oil

10 drops clary sage essential oil

40 drops lavender essential oil

40 drops lemon essential oil

10 drops thyme essential oil

herbs and flower petals for topping

1 Follow the detailed step-by-step instructions on page 25. Sieve the bicarbonate of soda, citric acid, and cornstarch together into a large mixing bowl.

2 Add the rosemary powder and mix in. If you only have the dried herb it is easy to grind to a powder in a coffee grinder. Spray on a fine mist of essential oils and mix well.

3 Continue spraying and mixing until the mixture just about holds together when you press a handful firmly between your fingers.

4 Place a sprinkling of dried herbs and flower petals in the bottom of each mold, then pack the mixture in tightly.

5 Press the two halves of the mold together and hold firmly with clips. If you do not have spherical molds, try using flexible rubber ice cube molds.

6 Leave the mixture for a few hours to harden then remove from the molds with a firm, twisting action. Allow a day for your bombes to dry, then they are ready to use and enjoy.

chamomile and cucumber

A gentle, relaxing soap for fair and sensitive skins with cooling cucumber and soothing chamomile.

ingredients

5 oz/145 g sodium hydroxide

13 oz/375 g spring water

1 lb 3 oz/600 g olive oil

10½ oz/300 g coconut oil

3½ oz/100 g borage oil

1 tsp/5 ml German chamomile essential oil

1½ tsp/7.5 ml juniper berry essential oil

1½ tsp/7.5 ml lemon essential oil

1 tbsp/15 ml cucumber extract

1 Follow the detailed step-by-step instructions on pages 20–21. Working in a well-ventilated place, carefully pour the sodium hydroxide into the spring water. Stir until fully dissolved then leave to cool.

2 Melt the olive, coconut, and borage oils in a large stainless steel pan. Remove the pan from the heat and carefully stir in the cooled lye solution. Using a slotted spoon, continue stirring to mix the lye and oils. The mixture will gradually thicken and trace.

3 When the soap mixture has traced, stir in the essential oils and cucumber extract. German chamomile is a dark blue color, so be careful of any spillages as it may stain. It will turn a subtle green in the soap mixture.

4 Pour the soap into your mold. Cover the mold with a blanket and set aside for 24–48 hours to cool completely.

5 When cool, turn out of the mold. Cut into bars and leave somewhere cool and airy to mature for 4–6 weeks before using.

basil and bergamot

Clear your mind and freshen your senses with an enlivening blend of basil and bergamot. A clear, green soap with a penetrating, herby aroma.

ingredients

2lb 2 oz/1 kg clear soap base pellets

1 tbsp/15 ml pumpkin oil

1 tsp/5 ml basil essential oil

1 tsp/5 ml bergamot essential oil

2 tsp/10 ml lavender essential oil

1 tbsp/15 ml calendula petals

4 tsp/20 ml dried basil leaves

1 Follow the detailed step-by-step instructions on page 23. Place the soap base pellets into the top half of a double boiler. If you are using a solid soap base, grate it first. Melt over a gentle heat.

2 Stir in the pumpkin oil then remove the pan from the heat and leave to cool for a few minutes. Stir in the essential oils and mix in well.

3 Coarsely grind the calendula petals and dried basil leaves, then stir them into the soap mixture. Pour the soap into your mold and leave to set.

4 After about an hour the soap will be ready to turn out of the mold and cut into bars. This soap does not need any further time to mature and it is ready to use straight away.

lemon thyme

The word thyme comes from the ancient Greek word *thymus*, meaning to perfume. Combined with lemon this makes a sweet-scented soap with strong anti-bacterial properties.

ingredients

2 lb 2oz/1 kg clear soap base pellets

2 tsp/10 ml yellow palm oil

1 tbsp/15 ml lemon essential oil

1 tsp/5 ml lemon thyme essential oil

4 tsp/20 ml dried thyme leaves

1 Follow the detailed step-by-step instructions on page 23. Place the soap base into the top half of a double boiler and slowly melt over a gentle heat.

2 When fully melted, add the yellow palm oil and stir in. Remove the pan from the heat and leave to cool for a few minutes. Stir in the essential oils and dried thyme leaves.

3 Pour the soap into your mold then, as the soap starts to cool and thicken, stir again to ensure that the thyme leaves are evenly distributed throughout the soap. If you do not restir the soap mixture, the thyme leaves will rise to the surface of the soap. This also looks attractive, so the choice is yours.

4 Once the soap has cooled and set you can turn it out of the mold, cut into bars, and use straight away.

spice

cleopatra's cream

A soap fit for a queen. Milk soaps are rich in vitamins and minerals to leave your skin feeling soft and beautifully conditioned. While ass milk may not be plentiful these days, goat's milk makes a wonderfully creamy soap.

ingredients

6 oz/175 g goats milk

7 oz/200 g spring water

5 oz/150 g sodium hydroxide

1 lb 1½ oz/500 g olive oil

14 oz/400 g coconut oil

3½ oz/100 g palm oil

1 tbsp/15 ml vanilla essential oil

1 tsp/5 ml vetivert essential oil

1 Follow the detailed step-by-step instructions on pages 20–21. Working in a well-ventilated place, mix the cold goat's milk and spring water together into a large heatproof cup or jug and place in a bowl of iced water.

2 Pour the sodium hydroxide into the milky water and stir until it is completely dissolved. Leave the cup or jug in the iced water to cool, stirring occasionally.

3 Melt the olive, coconut, and palm oils together in a large stainless steel pan over a low heat.

4 Remove the pan from the heat and carefully stir in the milky lye. Use a slotted spoon to stir and mix the soap. Continue stirring until the soap thickens and traces. The soap may give off an ammonia-like aroma, but don't worry this unpleasant scent will fade and disappear.

5 When the soap has traced, stir in the essential oils and pour into your molds.

6 Cover the molds with an old blanket and leave for a couple of days until the soap has completely cooled. Remove the soap from the mold and cut into bars. Leave somewhere cool and airy to harden and mature for 4–6 weeks. Your soap is ready to use.

cinnamon soap cakes

Easy-to-make soap cakes are an ideal way to turn leftover soap scraps, too small to use but too good to throw away, into luxurious, spicy, scented treats.

ingredients

2 lb 2 oz/1 kg leftover soap

1 tbsp/15 ml spring water

1 tsp/5 ml glycerine

½ tsp/2.5 ml cinnamon essential oil

1 tbsp/15 ml sweet orange essential oil

10 drops clove bud essential oil

1 Coarsely grate the leftover scraps of soap into a large mixing bowl. Add the spring water, glycerine, and essential oils and mix well.

2 Cover the bowl with a clean cloth and leave to stand for about 15 minutes, until the soap is slightly soft and pliable. If the soap you use for grating is fairly new, you may find that you do not need to leave it to soften.

3 Scoop up a handful of the mixture and press it firmly together. Push it firmly into your mold. If you do not have a suitable soap mold, you could simply roll your soap into a ball. The more you compress your mixture into the molds, the better your soap cakes will be.

4 Push out of the mold and stand your soap cakes somewhere to dry and harden. They should be ready to use in a day or two.

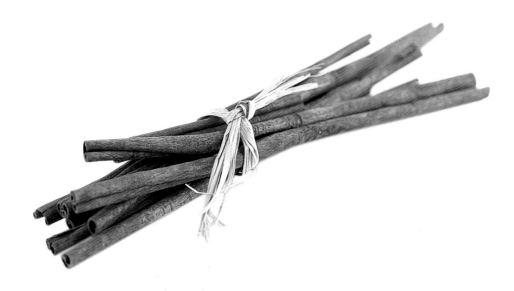

very vanilly

This soap blends the sweet, creamy scent of vanilla with cocoa butter for added richness and is dotted with ground coffee. This is an ideal kitchen soap, as coffee makes a very good deodorizer.

ingredients

4½ oz/130 g sodium hydroxide

13 oz/375 g spring water

1 lb 1½ oz/500 g olive oil

10½ oz/300 g palm oil

7 oz/200 g cocoa butter

1 tbsp/15 ml finely ground coffee

2 tsp/10 ml blue poppy seeds

4 tsp/20 ml vanilla absolute

1 Follow the detailed step-by-step instructions on pages 20–21. In a well-ventilated place, carefully pour the sodium hydroxide into the spring water and stir gently until fully dissolved. Set aside to cool.
2 Place the base oils into a large stainless steel pan and gently melt over a low heat. Remove the pan from the heat and stir in the cooled lye solution with a slotted spoon. Continue stirring to stop the lye and the oils separating and the mixture will gradually thicken and trace.
3 Remove a couple of spoonfuls of the plain mixture and put it into a separate bowl. You will use this to decorate the top of the soap. Remember to do this before adding your oils and botanicals, as the vanilla oil and ground coffee will turn your soap a warm, buttery brown color.
4 Add the ground coffee, poppy seeds, and vanilla absolute to the rest of the mixture and stir in thoroughly. Pour into your mold then swirl the plain mixture on top. Drag a knife through the soap mixture to create a decorative, marbled effect.
5 Wrap your mold in a blanket to insulate and help the soap to gel. Set aside for a couple of days until cool .You can now turn your soap out of the mold. Leave it somewhere cool and airy to mature and harden for 4–6 weeks before using.

orange and cinnamon

A sparkling champagne of citrus bubbles softened with milk powder and wheat germ flakes to make a bath bombe that will gently mull your bath water.

ingredients

1 lb/450 g bicarbonate of soda

10½ oz/300 g citric acid

5¼ oz/150 g cornstarch

2 tsp/10 ml milk powder

30 drops sweet orange essential oil

20 drops mandarin essential oil

10 drops cinnamon essential oil

1 tsp/5 ml cinnamon powder

1 tsp/5 ml wheat germ

1 tsp/5 ml turmeric

1 Follow the detailed step-by-step instructions on page 24. Sieve together the bicarbonate of soda, citric acid, cornstarch, and milk powder into a large mixing bowl.

2 Slowly and evenly spray on the essential oils, a little at a time and mixing thoroughly as you go. You only need a few drops of essential oil for each bombe you make.

3 Divide the mixture into three and mix the cinnamon and wheat germ into the first third, the turmeric into the second third, and leave the final third plain.

4 Pack alternate spoonfuls of the bombe mixture into your mold, pressing down firmly as you go. If you have used a round mold, press the two halves together and hold firmly in place with clips.

5 Leave for 3–4 hours to dry then remove from the mold with a firm twisting action. Store in a cool dry place and your bombes are ready to use in 24 hours, or as soon as they are fully hardened and dry.

christmas bath crystals

Carefully layered tiers of frankincense and myrrh make an enchanting gift. Add a sprinkling of crystals to your warm bath water to release magical scents of the East.

ingredients
1 lb 1½ oz/500 g Epsom salts
3½ oz/100 g frankincense tears
3½ oz/100 g myrrh tears
1 tsp/5 ml frankincense essential oil
1 tsp/5 ml myrrh essential oil

1 Fill a decorative bottle with alternate layers of Epsom salts, frankincense, and myrrh tears. Make sure that you pack each layer down firmly before adding the next. The end of a thick, long-handled wooden spoon makes an ideal packing tool. If you hold the bottle on its side while packing down the layers you can also create a spiral effect.

2 Fill the bottle to just below the neck then pour in the frankincense and myrrh oil. Seal the bottle and leave to infuse for a week before use.

clove and carnation

A spicy, floral combination of cloves and carnations, swirled with carnation and walnut leaves and topped with a row of clove buds.

ingredients

5¼ oz/150 g sodium hydroxide

13 oz/375 g spring water

14 oz/400 g olive oil

14 oz/400 g coconut oil

7 oz/200 g avocado oil

¾ tsp/3.75 ml carnation absolute

2 tsp/10ml geranium essential oil

1 tsp/5ml patchouli essential oil

15 drops clove bud essential oil

4 tsp/20 ml ground carnation leaves

1 tbsp/15 ml ground rosehips

2 tsp/10 ml ground walnut leaves

clove buds for topping

1 Follow the detailed step-by-step instructions on pages 20–21. In a well-ventilated place, carefully pour the sodium hydroxide into the spring water and stir gently until fully dissolved. Set aside to cool.

2 Melt the olive, coconut, and avocado oils in a large stainless steel pan over a gentle heat. Remove from the heat and carefully pour in the cooled lye solution. Stir with a slotted spoon to stop the oils and lye from separating.

3 Continue stirring and gradually the soap mixture will thicken and trace; this process may take a few hours. When the soap has traced, stir in the essential oils and mix in thoroughly.

4 Now add the carnation and walnut leaves and stir in. Finally, add the ground rosehips. These create the main color in your soap. Mix in unevenly to create a rippled, marble effect.

5 Pour your soap mixture into the mold. Insulate with a layer of blankets to help your soap mixture gel and leave covered for 24–48 hours until it has cooled. Turn out of the mold and leave somewhere cool and airy for around 4–6 weeks while your soap hardens and matures.

6 Cut into bars using a sharp knife and decorate the top with a row of clove buds.

honey ginger melts

The warm and inviting aroma of ginger and sandalwood in these massage melts is enriched with the sweetness of honey. Massage gently over tired muscles to stimulate circulation and melt away tension.

ingredients

9 oz/250 g dried chickpeas

7 oz/200 g cocoa butter

2 oz/50 g shea butter

2 oz/50 g beeswax

½ tsp/2.5 ml organic honey

¾ tsp/3.75 ml ginger essential oil

½ tsp/2.5 ml sandalwood essential oil

15 drops lemongrass essential oil

10 drops cinnamon essential oil

1 Scatter a layer of uncooked, dried chickpeas over the bottom of your mold. The chickpeas will have a gentle stimulating effect when rubbed firmly over your skin.

2 Follow the detailed step-by-step instructions on page 25. Melt the cocoa butter, shea butter, and beeswax in a small pan over a low heat. Add the honey and mix in thoroughly.

3 Remove the pan from the heat and allow to cool for a few minutes then stir in the essential oils. Carefully pour the mixture into the molds, covering the chickpeas.

4 Allow to cool and set, then put into the fridge until completely hard. Your melts will then pop easily out of the mold and are ready to use straight away.

winter rose

Clear, crisp, and bright, like roses on a winter morning. A fragrant, spiced soap, decorated with a spray of dried pink rose buds.

ingredients

5¼ oz/150 g sodium hydroxide

13 oz/375 g spring water

12 oz/350 g olive oil

14 oz/400 g coconut oil

2 oz/50 g rosehip oil

7 oz/200 g sweet almond oil

1 tsp/5 ml rose otto essential oil

1 tbsp/15 ml geranium essential oil

10 drops black pepper essential oil

10 drops nutmeg essential oil

2 tbsp/30 ml paprika

1 tbsp/15 ml cayenne

1 tsp/5 ml ground walnut leaves

1 Follow the detailed step-by-step instructions on pages 20–21. In a well-ventilated place, carefully pour the sodium hydroxide into the spring water and stir gently until fully dissolved. Set aside to cool.
2 Place all the base oils into a large stainless steel pan and slowly melt over a low heat. Remove the pan from the heat and carefully pour in the cooled lye solution. Stir with a slotted spoon and the mixture will thicken and trace.
3 Take out a couple of spoonfuls of the soap mixture and leave in a separate bowl. Add the essential oils and herbs and spices to the rest of the soap and mix in thoroughly.
4 Pour into your mold, then spoon the little bit of plain mixture you had set aside over the surface. Drag a knife back and forth through the surface of the soap to create a swirled effect.
5 Cover and insulate your mold with blankets to help the soap gel, then leave for a day or two until the soap has cooled.
6 Remove from the mold and stand somewhere cool and airy for 4–6 weeks while the soap cures. You can then cut it into bars and decorate with dried pink rose buds.

shea silk

Leave your skin feeling as soft as silk with this dreamy sweet massage melt, full of the alluring aroma of ylang ylang and the silky touch of shea butter.

ingredients

12 oz/350 g shea butter

2 oz/50 g white beeswax

2 oz/50 g yellow beeswax

1 tsp/5 ml ylang ylang essential oil

½ tsp/2.5 ml vetivert essential oil

½ tsp/2.5 ml tuberose essential oil

1 Follow the detailed step-by-step instructions on page 25. Place the shea butter and white beeswax in a small pan and melt over a low heat.
2 When fully melted, remove from the heat and stand aside for a few minutes to cool. Carefully pour a spoonful of the melted oils into decorative chocolate molds and leave to set.
3 Now add the yellow beeswax to the remaining melted oil to create a pale creamy color and reheat until all of the pellets are fully melted.
4 Once melted, remove the pan from the heat and stand aside to cool for a minute or two. Stir in the essential oils then pour the mixture into separate base molds.
5 When fully hardened and set, remove the melts from the base molds and the chocolate molds.
6 Stick the two shapes together with a little drop of melted oil and store somewhere cool until you are ready to use your melts.

frankincense and myrrh

This soap is warm, rich, and luxurious and full of festive cheer. It is topped with a crust of frankincense and myrrh tears that soften to the touch of warm water, releasing their mellow aroma.

ingredients

5 oz/145 g sodium hydroxide

13 oz/375 g spring water

14 oz/400 g olive oil

10½ oz/300 g coconut oil

7 oz/200 g shea butter

3½ oz/100 g sweet almond oil

2 tsp/10 ml frankincense essential oil

2 tsp/10 ml myrrh essential oil

2 tsp/10 ml frankincense powder

2 tsp/10 ml myrrh powder

frankincense and myrrh tears for topping

1 Follow the detailed step-by-step instructions on pages 20–21. In a well-ventilated place, carefully pour the sodium hydroxide into the spring water and stir gently until fully dissolved. Set aside to cool.

2 While your lye solution is cooling, melt your base oils in a large stainless steel pan over a gentle heat. Remove from the heat and pour in the cooled lye, stirring carefully all the time.

3 Continue stirring with a slotted spoon until the mixture thickens and traces, then add the essential oils and mix in thoroughly. Add the powdered frankincense and myrrh and stir. Don't mix too thoroughly at this stage and you will create a lovely marbled effect.

4 Pour the soap mixture into your molds. Sprinkle with a layer of frankincense and myrrh tears and gently press into the surface of the soap to form an attractive crust.

5 Cover your molds with a blanket and set aside for 24–48 hours to cool. Remove your soap from the molds and leave somewhere cool and airy for 4–6 weeks to harden and mature.

ginger grapefruit

Refreshing and spicy with a fresh, revitalizing scent. The muscle warming and toning effects of ginger and grapefruit make this a good liquid soap to use after playing sports.

ingredients

1 lb 1½ oz/500 g finely grated cold processed soap

2 cups/500 ml spring water

2 tsp/10 ml glycerine

1 tsp/5 ml vodka

1 tsp/5 ml ginger essential oil

2 tsp/10 ml grapefruit essential oil

1 Follow the detailed step-by-step instructions on page 22. Place the finely grated soap into the top half of a double boiler. Add the spring water and slowly melt over a gentle heat.

2 Remove from the heat and add the glycerine and vodka. Leave to cool for a minute or two before stirring in the essential oils.

3 Pour into pretty bottles and your soap is ready to use as soon as it is cool again.

myrrh and jasmine

The intense, rich, floral scent of jasmine blends with the creamy, mellow aroma of myrrh in this thick liquid soap with a touch of oriental charm.

ingredients

1 lb 1½ oz/500 g finely grated cold processed soap

2 cups/500 ml jasmine floral water

1 tsp/5 ml myrrh essential oil

1 tsp/5 ml jasmine essential oil

1 tsp/5 ml myrrh powder

1 Follow the detailed step-by-step instructions on page 22. Place the finely grated soap into the top half of a double boiler. Add the jasmine floral water and slowly melt over a gentle heat.
2 Stir until an even, creamy consistency then remove from the heat and leave for a couple of minutes.
3 Stir in the essential oils and myrrh powder and mix well. Pour into airtight bottles and your liquid soap is ready to use when cool.

Ylang ylang is known as poor man's jasmine, so if your budget does not stretch to jasmine essential oil, substitute ylang ylang extra for a similar scent.

woodland

green velvet

For velvety smooth skin, this massage melt uses a creamy combination of cocoa butter and pumpkin oil with the soft, mossy scent of petitgrain, oakmoss, and palmarosa.

ingredients

1 lb 1½ oz/500 g cocoa butter

2 tsp/10 ml pumpkin oil

½ tsp/2.5 ml petitgrain essential oil

30 drops oakmoss essential oil

1 tsp/5 ml palmarosa essential oil

sprigs of lady's mantle

1 Follow the detailed step-by-step instructions on page 25. Melt the cocoa butter in a medium-sized pan over a low heat.

2 Add the pumpkin oil and warm through. The pumpkin will change your mixture to a warm green color. You can, if you wish, adjust the color by adding a touch more, or less, pumpkin oil.

3 When fully melted, remove the pan from the heat and stand aside for a couple of minutes to allow the mixture to cool slightly.

4 Stir in the essential oils then carefully pour the mixture into the molds. Individual yogurt pots or chocolate molds make attractive shapes.

5 Place in a fridge to set firm, then pop out of the mold and decorate with a sprig of lady's mantle (Alchemilla mollis) or another tiny, decorative herb.

oakmoss and
patchouli

A traditional chypre-style perfume with a tenacious, woody, masculine scent. The high lathering base oils make this a perfect shaving soap, with lots of soft bubbles.

ingredients

5¼ oz/150 g sodium hydroxide

13 oz/375 g spring water

1 lb 1½ oz/500 g coconut oil

10½ oz/300 g olive oil

7 oz/200 g castor oil

½ tsp/2.5 ml oakmoss essential oil

1 tsp/5 ml patchouli essential oil

1½ tsp/7.5 ml lavender essential oil

1 tsp/5 ml bergamot essential oil

1 Follow the detailed step-by-step instructions on pages 20–21. In a well-ventilated place, carefully add the sodium hydroxide to the spring water and stir gently until fully dissolved. Set aside to cool.
2 Melt the coconut oil in a large stainless steel pan and then add the olive oil and castor oil and warm through. Remove from the heat and carefully pour in the cooled lye solution.
3 Stir with a slotted spoon to stop the oils and lye solution separating. Continue stirring and gradually the mixture will thicken and trace. This process may take a few hours.
4 When traced, stir in the essential oils and mix well. Pour the soap mixture into an earthenware bowl or other suitable shaving dish.
5 Cover with a blanket to insulate the soap and help it gel. Leave for 24–48 hours to cool. Remove the blankets and leave somewhere cool and airy for around 4–6 weeks while your soap hardens and matures.

soap stone

This is a soap to soak away the strains of the day – smooth, soft, and rounded with a subtle marble and a soothing, mellow scent.

ingredients
5½ oz/155 g sodium hydroxide
13 oz/375 g spring water
1 lb 1½ oz/500 g olive oil
1 lb 1½ oz/500 g coconut oil
2 tsp/10 ml vetivert essential oil
2 tsp/10 ml ylang ylang essential oil
40 drops rose otto essential oil
2 tsp/10 ml paprika

1 Follow the detailed step-by-step instructions on pages 20–21. In a well-ventilated place, carefully add the sodium hydroxide to the spring water and stir gently until fully dissolved. Set aside to cool.

2 Place the olive and coconut oils into a large stainless steel pan and melt over a low heat. When fully melted, remove the pan from the heat and carefully pour in the lye solution, stirring all the time with a slotted spoon.

3 As you continue stirring, the mixture will gradually thicken and trace. Pour in the essential oils and mix in thoroughly.

4 Sprinkle on the paprika powder and swirl in to create a marbled effect. Pour the soap into your molds and cover with an old towel or blanket to help the soap gel.

5 Leave for 24–48 hours until the soap is completely cool, then remove from the mold and leave somewhere cool and airy to cure and mature for 4–6 weeks before using.

sandalwood
and walnut

Wonderfully rounded, soft, sweet, and woody, sandalwood needs little accompaniment. Distilled from the heartwood of 30-year-old trees, it has been used as a perfume for over 4000 years.

ingredients

2 lb 2 oz/1 kg clear soap base pellets

1 tsp/5 ml pumpkin oil

1 tsp/5 ml walnut oil

1 tsp/5 ml turmeric

4 tsp/20 ml sandalwood essential oil

2 tbsp/30 ml ground walnut leaves

1 Follow the detailed step-by-step instructions on page 23. Place the clear soap base into the top half of a double boiler. Soap pellets melt quickly, but a solid soap base is just as easy if you grate it first.
2 Melt the soap base over a low heat. Add the pumpkin and walnut oils together with the turmeric powder and stir in thoroughly. The soap base will turn a rich, deep amber-brown color.
3 Remove the pan from the heat and set aside for a minute or two to cool. Stir in the essential oils and walnut leaves then pour the mixture into your mold.
4 If the soap is still quite warm, the walnut leaves will rise to the surface of the mixture. Leave another minute or two, then, as the soap starts to thicken, stir again to ensure that the walnut leaves are evenly distributed throughout the soap.
5 The soap is ready to pop out of the mold, cut, and use in just an hour or two, or as soon as it is completely cool.

green tea

This clear soap, infused with a rich, honey, tea-like scent, is plain and simple, decorated with the warm tones of autumn leaves.

ingredients

2 lb 2 oz/1 kg clear soap base

4 tsp/20 ml green tea

40 drops helichrysm absolute

1 tsp/5 ml Roman chamomile essential oil

1 tbsp/15 ml lemon essential oil

autumn leaves for decoration

1 Follow the detailed step-by-step instructions on page 23. Melt the soap base in the top half of a double boiler over a low heat. Soap pellets melt quickly, but if you are using a solid soap base, grate it first.

2 Tie the green tea in a cheesecloth (muslin) bag and put it into the melted soap mixture. Leave on a very low heat for about half an hour for the tea to infuse. Check and stir occasionally to ensure that the melted soap does not stick or burn.

3 The soap mixture will take on a lovely, delicate, tea-like color. When the desired color is reached, take out the cheesecloth (muslin) bag and discard.

4 Remove the pan from the heat and set aside to cool a little before adding the essential oils to the soap mixture, stirring in thoroughly.

5 Pour a thin layer of soap over the bottom of your mold. Carefully arrange the dried leaves on top and press down into the soap mixture. Leave for a minute or two then carefully spoon a layer of soap over the top, making sure that the leaves are well covered.

6 Wait another minute or two, then pour the rest of the soap mixture over the top. Waiting between layers ensures that the soap mixture does not remelt with the heat of the next layer and the leaves remain held in place.

7 Leave to cool for a couple of hours and remove from the mold as soon as your soap is set. It is ready to use.

juniper pine

A soap with the forest fresh fragrance of juniper and pine, marbled with spike lavender and set on a bed of juniper berries. Spike lavender has a more pungent, camphoraceous note than true lavender.

ingredients

4½ oz/130 g sodium hydroxide

13 oz/375 g spring water

1 lb 3 oz/600 g olive oil

5¼ oz/150 g sweet almond oil

9 oz/250 g palm oil

1 tsp/5 ml juniper berry essential oil

30 drops pine essential oil

2 tsp/10 ml spike lavender essential oil

1 tsp/5 ml lemon essential oil

¼ tsp/1.25 ml indigo powder

dried juniper berries for topping

1 Follow the detailed step-by-step instructions on pages 20–21. In a well-ventilated place, carefully add the sodium hydroxide to the spring water and stir gently until fully dissolved. Set aside to cool.

2 Melt the olive, sweet almond, and palm oils together in a large stainless steel pan over a gentle heat. Remove the pan from the heat and carefully stir in the lye solution. Use a slotted spoon and continue stirring to fully incorporate the mixture.

3 After a while the mixture will thicken and trace. You can then add the essential oils and stir in thoroughly.

4 Sprinkle on the indigo powder and mix in unevenly to create a marbled effect. Be careful to use only a tiny amount of indigo powder, otherwise the lather will be blue.

5 Line the bottom of your mold with a layer of juniper berries, then carefully pour the soap mixture on top. Insulate the mold with a blanket and leave the soap to gel for 24–48 hours.

6 When the soap has fully cooled, remove the covers and turn the soap out of the mold. Stand the soap somewhere cool and airy for around 4–6 weeks before using.

wood violets

Let your senses drift through the enchanting scents of woodland flowers with this heady soap evoking the deep, dark, and alluring perfume of violets under a midnight moon

ingredients

4½ oz/130 g sodium hydroxide

13 oz/375 g spring water

1 lb 3 oz/600 g olive oil

3½ oz/100 g avocado oil

10½ oz/300 g palm oil

1 tsp/5 ml violet leaf essential oil

1 tsp/5 ml vetivert essential oil

2 tsp/10 ml patchouli essential oil

½ tsp/2.5 ml geranium essential oil

4 tsp/20 ml alkanet

1 tsp/5 ml cinnamon powder

1 tsp/5 ml paprika powder

1 Follow the detailed step-by-step instructions on pages 20–21. In a well-ventilated place, carefully add the sodium hydroxide to the spring water and stir gently until fully dissolved. Set aside to cool.

2 Melt the olive, avocado, and palm oils in a large, stainless steel pan over a gentle heat. Remove the pan from the heat and carefully pour in the lye solution. Stir with a slotted spoon to stop the oils and lye from separating.

3 Continue stirring and gradually the mixture will thicken and trace. Pour in the essential oils and mix well. Add the alkanet and half the cinnamon and stir. There is no need to be too thorough when mixing as a slight variation in tone and color will look attractive.

4 Pour about half the mixture into your mold then sprinkle the rest of the cinnamon powder over the surface of your soap and swirl with a knife.

5 Add the paprika to the remainder of your soap mixture and stir in, again not too thoroughly. Pour this soap mixture into your mold, swirl again then cover with blankets and insulate the mold to help the soap gel. Leave to cool for 24–48 hours.

6 Remove the soap from the mold, cut into bars, and leave somewhere cool and airy for around 4–6 weeks to harden and mature before using.

milkwood

A creamy, moisturizing milk soap. Soothing and gentle, full of skin nourishing properties, and mild enough for young skins.

ingredients

5 oz/145 g sodium hydroxide

13 oz/375 g spring water

1 lb 5 oz/700 g olive oil

10½ oz/300 g coconut oil

2½ tsp/12.5 ml patchouli essential oil

1½ tsp/7.5 ml myrrh essential oil

1 tsp/5 ml neroli essential oil

15 drops clary sage essential oil

1 tbsp/15 ml milk powder

1 Follow the detailed step-by-step instructions on pages 20–21. Working in a well-ventilated place, carefully pour the sodium hydroxide into the spring water, stirring until completely dissolved. Set aside to cool.

2 Melt the olive and coconut oils in a large stainless steel pan over a gentle heat. Remove the pan from the heat and pour in the cooled lye solution, stirring gently all the time with a slotted spoon.

3 Continue stirring and the soap mixture will eventually thicken and trace. Add the essential oils and mix in thoroughly. Finally, sprinkle on the milk powder and stir in well.

4 Pour the mixture into your mold. Cover with a blanket and set aside for 24–48 hours to cool. Remove from the mold. Cut into bars and leave in a cool and airy place for around 4–6 weeks to fully harden and mature before using.

tea tree and eucalyptus

The cleansing, clearing, and medicated scent of tea tree is teamed with eucalyptus. Tea tree has very powerful anti-bacterial, anti-viral, and anti-fungal properties, making this an ideal soap for teenage skins.

ingredients

5 oz/145 g sodium hydroxide

13 oz/375 g spring water

14 oz/400 g olive oil

10½ oz/300 g coconut oil

9 oz/250 g palm oil

2 oz/50 g shea butter

2½ tsp/12.5 ml tea tree essential oil

2½ tsp/12.5 ml eucalyptus essential oil

2 tsp/10 ml ground parsley leaves

2 tsp/10 ml ground rosemary leaves

1 Follow the detailed step-by-step instructions on pages 20–21. In a well-ventilated place, carefully add the sodium hydroxide to the spring water and stir gently until fully dissolved. Set aside to cool.

2 Melt the base oils in a large stainless steel pan. Remove the pan from the heat and carefully pour in the lye solution. Stir continuously with a slotted spoon to stop the oils and lye separating.

3 Continue stirring until the soap mixture thickens and traces. Add the essential oils and mix in thoroughly.

4 Pour most of the soap mixture into your molds, keeping back the last couple of spoonfuls for the topping.

5 Stir the ground parsley and rosemary leaves into the last measure of soap mixture. Swirl this on top of the rest of the soap in the mold. Drag a knife through the mixture in a wavy motion to create a decorative effect.

6 Cover and insulate the mold with blankets to help the soap to gel. Leave to cool for 24–48 hours. Remove the soap from the mold and stand it somewhere cool and airy to harden and mature for 4–6 weeks before using.

wood sprite

Fill your bath with a fantasy of bubbles. These softly scented, pebble-like bombes are filled with the woodland scent of lavender, sandalwood, and black pepper.

ingredients

1 lb/450g bicarbonate of soda
10½ oz/300 g citric acid
5¼ oz/150 g cornstarch
5 drops black pepper essential oil
1 tsp/5 ml lavender essential oil
½ tsp/2.5 ml sandalwood essential oil
1 tsp/5 ml alkanet
1 tsp/5 ml rosemary
½ tsp/2.5 ml cinnamon
½ tsp/2.5 ml turmeric

1 Follow the detailed step-by-step instructions on page 24. Sieve the bicarbonate of soda, citric acid, and cornstarch together into a large mixing bowl.
2 Slowly and evenly spray on the essential oils, carefully mixing in as you go. Be careful not to spray on too much; you only need a tiny quantity of essential oils. The mixture is ready when it just about holds together when pressed firmly between your fingers.
3 Divide the bombe mixture into five portions and color each portion with a different herb (alkanet, rosemary, cinnamon, and turmeric), leaving the last portion plain white.
4 Pack alternate spoonfuls of the mixture into your molds, pressing down firmly as you go. Press the two halves of the molds together and hold in place with clips.
5 Leave for a few hours to harden, preferably overnight, then remove the bombes from the molds with a firm twisting action.
6 Store in a cool dry place. Your bombes are ready to use in a couple of days, as soon as they have fully hardened and dried.

lemon eucalyptus

A slightly astringent and medicated liquid soap with the clean and clearing scent of lemon and eucalyptus. An ideal cleanser for oily skins.

ingredients

1 lb 1½ oz/500 g finely grated cold processed soap

1 tsp/5 ml yellow palm oil

2 cups/500 ml spring water

1½ tsp/7.5 ml lemon essential oil

20 drops lemon eucalyptus essential oil

1 Follow the detailed step-by-step instructions on page 22. Place the finely grated soap and palm oil in the top half of a double boiler over a gentle heat. Add the spring water and mix in until the liquid soap is of an even consistency. You can adjust the thickness of your liquid soap by adding more or less water.

2 Remove from the heat and allow to cool for a couple of minutes before stirring in the essential oils.

3 Pour into airtight bottles and leave the liquid soap to cool completely. You can use the soap immediately.

wintergreen

Imagine misty, mellow, winter mornings, tendrils of green ivy and damp moss underfoot. That's the soft and rounded scent of wintergreen.

ingredients

1 lb 1½ oz/500 g finely grated cold processed soap

2 cups/500 ml spring water

40 drops mimosa essential oil

20 drops oakmoss essential oil

½ tsp/2.5 ml sandalwood essential oil

½ tsp/2.5 ml vetivert essential oil

40 drops ylang ylang essential oil

2 tsp/10 ml pumpkin oil

1 tsp/5 ml yellow palm oil

4 tsp/20 ml condensed cold tea

1 Follow the detailed step-by-step instructions on page 22. Mix the finely grated soap in the top half of a double boiler with the spring water. Melt over a gentle heat and stir until the mixture is of a thick, even consistency.

2 Remove from the heat and allow to cool for a couple of minutes before adding the essential oils.

3 Divide the mixture into three. Add the pumpkin oil to one third, the yellow palm oil to the second third, and the cold, condensed tea to the final third.

4 When completely cool, pour each third, one after the other, into a decorative bottle to create a soft, cloudy, marbled effect.

5 If the bottle is shaken vigorously the colors will, of course, mix together but, just left standing, the ripple of colors should remain as this liquid soap is quite thick.

finishing touches

Each of the recipes in this book will give you enough for around ten bars of soap, so you will very quickly have lots of soap to give away. If you want to plan ahead for a special occasion and need to store your soaps, simply wrap them in greaseproof paper and leave them somewhere cool and dry. The back of a closet or the bottom of a drawer is ideal. Away from the light and heat, you will preserve the freshness of their color and scent and, as they mature and age, your bars will harden and improve in quality. You will also find their delicate perfume permeating whatever else is stored with them, so carefully hide them among your clothes and linens to leave them beautifully scented. When made correctly, your soap should keep in pristine condition for a year or more, so you will always have a ready supply of last-minute gifts made, plus of course, plenty left over for your own personal use.

Your bombes, too, should also store for some months. An airtight tin is ideal, as this will stop them absorbing any moisture from the air and softening. Melts are best made a little nearer the time you wish to use them. They are vulnerable to high temperatures and are best made,

at most, only a few weeks in advance, but as they are so quick and easy to make, this shouldn't pose too much of a problem. Handmade soaps, bombes, and melts make perfect presents and will always be a very welcome and popular gift. Continue the natural feel by wrapping your presents in cheesecloth (muslin) or handmade paper and tying with raffia or string. For the finishing touch, tie with a posy of dried flowers, leaves, grasses, and seed heads, or glue on an arrangement of hips, berries, and shells.

For a more rustic look, you can even decorate the soaps themselves by pressing petals directly into their surface before they have fully hardened. The decoration may have to be removed before the soap is used but they do enhance the natural feel of soaps. This process works well for melts too. Festive gifts look great tied with cinnamon sticks, dried citrus slices, cones, and nuts. Whatever the season, you will find no shortage of seedpods and flower heads to make your gifts look special and unique. Above all, enjoy the creative process and make your soaps, bath bombes, and massage melts distinctive in their own way and individual to you.

glossary

absolute a highly concentrated viscous oil, typically produced by solvent extraction from the plant material.

base oils The fatty, dense, non-volatile plant and vegetable oils that make up the body of the soap. Oils can be liquid, like olive oil, or solid, like cocoa butter.

botanicals herbs, spices, and flower petals added to soap to create texture, color, and enhance scent.

cold processed traditional method of producing soap. An alkali and a fat are combined to form glycerine and a sodium salt of the fatty acid, in other words, soap.

cure process of hardening and maturing soap. Newly unmolded, cold processed soap will still be a little harsh, and the texture too soft, to use. Left somewhere cool and airy to cure for a period of 4–6 weeks, the soap will harden and the pH level will drop.

double boiler A type of saucepan which has a smaller pan sitting inside a larger pan. The larger, base pan is filled with water which, when warmed gently melts, without risk of burning, the ingredients placed in the top pan.

emollient something that softens and smoothes the skin.

epsom salts magnesium sulphate. A mineral salt originally found in Epsom, Surrey, UK. Excellent for relieving tired and aching muscles when added to baths.

essential oil a volatile, aromatic oil, extracted from the flowers, leaves, bark, and roots of plants. Often attributed with many medicinal and therapeutic properties, as well as a pleasing aroma.

exfoliant a substance that is effective in removing the outer layer of dead skin cells.

expressed method of extracting essential oils from citrus fruits by use of pressure. Once done by hand, now carried out by use of centrifugal force.

FCF furocoumarin free oil.

fixative a material that slows down the rate of evaporation of a more volatile oil.

furocoumarins chemical constituent of some essential oils. Certain furocoumarins, namely bergapten, have been found to be photo toxic on human skin. Always use furocoumarin free oil.

gel a stage of soap making. If newly traced soap is well insulated, the soap mixture will super heat and turn to a clear, jelly-like consistency, taking a couple of days to return to its solid, opaque form.

humectant a substance that absorbs and promotes the retention of moisture from the air.

lye a concentrated solution of sodium hydroxide and water.

macerated softened or separated as a result of soaking.

oil mister a fine mist sprayer, often used in cooking for spraying on a fine, even mist of oil, over salads for instance.

olfaction the sense of smell.

pH a measure of acidity or alkalinity. Soap is always alkaline.

photo toxic substance that causes sensitization and skin pigmentation when exposed to direct sunlight. Can cause permanent scaring.

pomace the final pressing of olive oil from the remaining skin and pits.

saponify to undergo a process by which a fat is converted into soap by means of an alkali.

saponins found in a small group of plants that have a steroid structure that foam when shaken.

seized an undesirable state of soap making, producing a coarse, lumpy, poorly mixed soap. Over-hot base oils or lye solution will cause seizing, as will insufficient stirring. Certain essential oils are also renowned for seizing soap too.

soap base a clear or opaque, premade soap that simply requires melting before adding scent and botanicals, then allowing to reset.

sodium hydroxide (NaOH) a white, strongly alkaline solid used in the production of cold processed soap.

solvent extracted method of extracting essential oils by which the plant material is soaked in a solvent. The solvent is then removed to leave th essential oil. Suitable for very delicate blooms and creates a very true to nature oil.

steam distilled process of extraction of essential oils. Steam is passed through the plant material, soaking up the essential oil. This steam is then condensed to leave the water with the essential oil floating on the top.

tea infusion a herbal solution obtained by steeping the plant material in water.

trace stage at which soap is ready to pour into a mold. Distinguished by a visible trail left and lasting for a couple of seconds when a spoon is dragged through the soap mixture.

unsaponifiable unable to turn to soap. A small percentage of unsaponified oils in your soap are highly desirable, as it is these that will create a moisturizing bar. Too high a percentage of unsaponifiables will make your soap feel greasy.

volatile unstable and evaporates quickly, as in essential oils.

suppliers

UK

Fred Aldous Ltd
37 Lever Street, Manchester, M1 1LW
tel: 0161 236 2477 website: www.fredaldous.co.uk
email: aldous@btinternet.com
glycerine soap base, molds.

G Baldwin and Co
173 Walworth Road, London SE17 1RW
tel: 020 7703 5550 website: www. baldwins.co.uk
email: sales@baldwins.co.uk
dried herbs, essential oils, base oils.

Elixarome Ltd
Hop Pocket Lane, Paddock Wood, Tonbridge,
Kent TN12 6DQ
tel: 01892 833334 website: www.aroma-oils.co.uk
email: oils@aroma-oils.co.uk
pure essential oils, floral waters and base oils.

Essentially Oils Ltd
Unit 8/10 Mount Farm, Junction Road, Churchill Chipping
Norton, Oxfordshire OX7 6NP
tel: 01608 659544 fax: 01608 659566
website: www.essentiallyoils.com

Hobbycraft
For directions to your nearest Hobbycraft store and for
opening hours please call 0800 027 2387
website: www.hobbycraft.co.uk

Neal's Yard Remedies
15 Neal's Yard, Covent Garden, London WC2H 9DP
tel: 020 7379 7222 website: www.nealsyardremedies.com
email: mail@nealsyardremedies.com
essential oils, base oils, dried herbs.

Merrywood
The Street, Mereworth, Kent ME18 5NA
tel: 01622 812755 website: www.merrywood.co.uk
email: thesoapfactory@merrywood.co.uk
*herbs, spices and flower petals, many of which are organically
grown plus base oils and molds.*

USA

Rainbow Meadow Inc
Po Box 457, Napoleon, MI 49261
tel: 517-817-0021 1-800-207-4047 toll free US and Canada
website: www.rainbowmeadow.com
email: rainbowmeadow@ameritech.net
soap making supplies, oils, essential oils, botanicals and molds.

Milky Way Molds Inc
PMB#473, 4326 SE Woodstock
Portland, OR97206
tel: 1-800-227-4530 website: www.milkywaymolds.com
email: info@milkywaymolds.com
molds suitable for both cold processed and melt and pour soaps.

San Francisco Herb Co
250 14th Street, San Francisco
CA 94103
tel: 800-227-4530 or 415-861-7174
website: www.sfherb.com email: info@sfherb.com
herbs, spices and flower petals, essential oils.

Sweetcakes
6020 Blue Circle Dr., Minnetonka, MN 55343
tel: 952-945-9900 website: www.sweetcakes.com
email: info@sweetcakes.com
*essential oils, base oils, melt and pour soap bases, a unique range
of molds.*

AUSTRALIA

Select Botanicals
53 College Street, Gladesville
NSW 2111 tel: 02 9817 0400 fax: 02 9817 0500
email: info@selectbotanicals.com.au
www.selectbotanicals.com.au   *essential oils.*

Springfields Aromatherapy
Unit 2, 2 Anella Avenue
Castle Hill, NSW 2154 tel: 02 9894 9933
fax: 02 9894 0199 email: sales@springfieldsaroma.com
website: www.springfieldsaroma.com *essential oils, base oils.*

CANADA

Aquarius Aromatherapy & Soap
31 32929 Mission Way,
Mission B.C. tel: 604 826 4199 fax: 604 826 3322
website: aquariusaroma-soap.com
email: inquiries@aquariusaroma-soap.com
essential oils, soapmaking kits, molds, carrier oils, soap bases.

The Aromatherapy Shoppe
At the Market Square,
2109 Ottawa Street, Windsor, Ontario NBY 1R8
tel: 519 253 6595 fax: 519 966 3404
website: www.windsor.igs.net email: aromatic@windsor.igs.net
essential oils, carrier oils, shampoos, skin creams.

Essential Botanicals
Order Desk: 1-888-327-1874
fax: 519 824-8017 www.essentialbotanicals.com
essential oils, flower waters.

Plant Life
17 Lesley Street, Box 133, Toronto, Ontario M4M3H9
tel: 888 690-4820 fax: 416 466 6458
website: www.plant-life.com email: info@plant-life.com
flower waters.

Poya Natural Inc.
21-B Regan Road, Brampton, Ontario L7A 1C5
tel: 905 840-5459 fax: 905 846-1784
Order desk: 1-8777-255-7692
website: www.poyanaturals.com email: oils@poyanaturals.com
essential oils, bottles, shea butter, citric acid.

index

acknowledgments

AUTHOR'S ACKNOWLEDGMENTS

I will always have fond memories of finishing the final draft of this book whilst on holiday in the French Alps. Those clear, blue, glacial rivers and alpine meadows are etched deep in my psyche. I didn't do my fair share of chores that holiday, sloping off at every opportunity to keep company with my laptop, lost amid thoughts of exotic soaps and evocative scents. I would like to thank everybody who waited on me, making sure my wine glass was always refilled.

Being given the opportunity to write this book has been a privileged experience and, having now realised what is involved I have come to the conclusion that it shouldn't be just my name on the front cover but the long list of the designers, photographers, editors and proof readers etc. that all make up the very talented Collins and Brown team. Some of you are mentioned on the inside cover, some of you are not. To you all, a very big thank you for turning a dream into a reality.

Thanks should also go to Wendy who checked through the final draft and whose horticultural knowledge far outstrips mine, and to Patty who came to my rescue with her knowledge of the other side of the pond and who provided the inspiration for the Oakmoss and Patchouli recipe.

Biggest thanks of all though must go to Simon. Thank you.

PUBLISHER'S ACKNOWLEDGMENTS

Thank you to The White Company for the kind loan of their products. To request a catalogue call 0870 900 9555 or visit www.thewhiteco.com.

All photographs by Siân Irvine except for that on page 7, by Steve Wooster.

bibliography

Lawless, Julia, *The Encyclopaedia of Essential Oils*, (HarperCollins, 2002)

McVicar, Jekka, *Jekka's Complete Herb Book*, (Kyle Cathie, 2001)

Mabey, Richard, *Flora Britannica*, (Sinclair-Stevenson, 1996)

Phillips, Roger and Foy, Nicky, *Herbs* (Pan, 1990)

Wildwood, Chrissie, *Bloomsbury Encyclopedia of Aromatherapy*, (Bloomsbury, 1996)

conversion chart

Always use either metric or imperial meausurements only in a recipe. These conversions are approximate and have been rounded up or down.

weight		volume	
25 g	1 oz	20 ml	$\frac{3}{5}$ fl oz
50 g	2 oz	30 ml	1 fl oz
75 g	3 oz	60 ml	2 fl o z
110 g	4 oz	75 ml	$2\frac{1}{2}$ fl oz
175 g	6 oz	90 ml	3 fl oz
225 g	8 oz	150 ml	5 fl oz ($\frac{1}{4}$ pint)
275 g	10 oz	175 ml	6 fl oz
350 g	12 oz	250 ml	8 fl oz
400 g	14 oz	300 ml	10 fl oz ($\frac{1}{2}$ pint)
500 g	1 lb 1 oz	400 ml	13 fl oz
		450 ml	15 fl oz ($\frac{3}{4}$ pint)
		600 ml	20 fl oz (1 pint)